The Only True History of Lizzie Finn
The Steward of Christendom
White Woman Street

The Steward of Christendom
'No piece of theatre yet seen on the Irish stage has presented the
viewpoint of the Irish Catholic loyalist of eighty years ago with such
acute sensitivity, such marvellous intellectual, historical and
dramatic integrity . . . This is a quite wonderful play which
brilliantly re-opens a hitherto closed chapter of Irish history. It is
lyrical and profound, extremely funny and extraordinarily
observant; and above all it is hauntingly sad. This is one of the
great Irish tragedies, and all the more tragic because true.'

Kevin Myers, *Irish Times*

'The strengths of this latest piece . . . establish Barry as a dramatist
of the finest sort.'

Jeremy Kingston, *Times*

'An outstanding new play . . . in [which] his poetic and dramatic
gifts achieve a resonant harmony.'

Michael Billington, *Guardian*

White Woman Street
'Weaving together a Western, a haunting myth-like story, and a
very Irish drama of exile (all the characters have a keen sense of
being culturally displaced), the play is engrossing. . . . Barry's
strength as a dramatist is best observed in the way he makes tragic
and comic feeling grate against each other.'

Independent

'His writing is tense with feeling and intelligence and a sense of
subdued ferocity.'

Sunday Times

Sebastian Barry was born in Dublin in 1955 where he still lives.
He was elected to Aosdana in 1989 and was Ansbacher Writer-in-
Residence at the Abbey Theatre, Dublin in 1990. His other plays
include *The Pentagonal Dream* (Damer Theatre, Dublin, 1986); *Boss
Grady's Boys* (Abbey Theatre, Peacock stage, Dublin, 1988) which
won the first BBC/Steward Parker Award; and *Prayers of Sherkin*
(Abbey Theatre, Peacock stage, Dublin, 1990). He has also
published several works of poetry and fiction.

by the same author

**Prayers of Sherkin
Boss Grady's Boys**

The Only True History of Lizzie Finn
The Steward of Christendom
White Woman Street

Three plays by
Sebastian Barry

Methuen Drama

Methuen Modern Plays

First published in Great Britain 1995
by Methuen Drama
an imprint of Reed International Books Ltd
Michelin House, 81 Fulham Road, London SW3 6RB
and Auckland, Melbourne, Singapore and Toronto
and distributed in the United States of America
by Heinemann, a division of Reed Elsevier Inc.
361 Hanover Street, Portsmouth, New Hampshire 03801 3959

Reprinted 1996

ISBN 0 413 69890 4

Introduction
Grace and Disgrace

In Sebastian Barry's luminous plays, grace and disgrace are
not opposites but constant companions. His people are, in the
eyes of their time, disgraceful. The central characters of these
plays are, respectively, a desperado, an enforcer for a
discredited regime and an exotic dancer. They are misfits,
anomalies, outlanders. Yet each is also marked by an amazing
grace. They are, in the mundane meaning of grace, possessed
in their different ways of extraordinary emotional elegance.
And they are also, in the religious sense, full of grace, touched
by some kind of inexplicable tenderness that rescues them
from oblivion and grants them an equivocal but unmistakable
blessing.

Sebastian Barry's plays are about history, but not in any
very obvious or familiar sense. Much of Irish theatre since
Sean O'Casey has had a direct relationship to public events.
Either directly or indirectly virtually all of the major plays
written in Ireland this century have reflected on the large-
scale public conflicts that have shaped individual destinies on
the island. First the conflict between Britishness and Irishness
(or Protestantism and Catholicism) and then the conflict
between tradition and modernity in independent Ireland
echoed through the theatre. The plays themselves tended,
inevitably, to be full of the resounding clash of epic forces. We
came to expect an especially turbulent kind of drama in
Ireland, and we were not disappointed.

Sebastian Barry's extraordinary theatrical history of
anomalous people, sustained now over five plays (*Boss Grady's
Boys* and *Prayers of Sherkin*, both published in 1991 as well as
the three collected here) marks a striking departure from these
precedents. By the late 1980s, when he found his voice in the
theatre, the old conflicts were losing their grip. On the one
hand, the contest between Britishness and Irishness had run
itself into the barren and blood-soaked ground of sectarian
strife in Northern Ireland. On the other, the epic clash of
tradition and modernity in the Republic of Ireland was

becoming an unequal match. Insofar as it still exists, traditional Ireland is alienated, angular and embattled, as strange, with its moving statues and paranoid visions, as any avant garde has ever been. Its image in the theatre is no longer the proud, confident, dangerous Bull McCabe of John B. Keane's *The Field*, but Barry's odd, sad, comic, encircled Boss Grady's Boys, holed up and waiting for death.

Such a vision of traditional Ireland cannot be the source of great, sweeping dramatic confrontations, and there was every reason to believe that Irish theatre would gradually dwindle. That it has instead found a new way of being alive on stage, a new source of theatrical power that does not depend on outward epic conflict, is Sebastian Barry's mighty achievement. In these plays, external conflict is almost entirely absent. They are, like the great plays of the Irish revival in the early part of this century, essentially poetic, relying on the power of theatre to evoke a world through language rather than assert it through action.

And they are that oddest and most unexpected of things at the end of the twentieth century – works of great formal beauty. They persuade and hold their audience, not through naturalistic illusions, baroque displays of emotion or titanic struggles of historic forces, but through containing all their turbulences within the most delicate and poised of structures, an invisible scaffolding of words and syntax. These plays happen in the space between the ordered serenity of the language on the one hand and the instability of the world in which they are spoken on the other.

In this, Barry is much closer to, say, William Butler Yeats than he is to the Irish playwrights of the 1960s and 1970s. These plays could almost have the same opening line as Yeats's *At the Hawk's Well*, 'I call to the eye of the mind . . .', for they have a ritual quality of evocation, of spirits called up before our eyes rather than invented from moment to moment on the stage. It is significant that most of the plays are prefigured in Sebastian Barry's slim volume of poems *Fanny Hawke Goes to the Mainland Forever*, published in 1989. Barry's original impulse is poetic, and that impulse carries through in the sheer depth of language in the plays, and in their linguistic containment of violent feeling, so reminiscent of Wordsworth's description of poetry as 'emotion recollected in tranquillity'. The language of the plays is tough, lucid and superbly theatrical, but it always retains that remarkable linguistic tranquillity that makes them poetic.

This not to say that Sebastian Barry's plays are refined creations from which the roughage of time and place, of Irish history and Irish land, have been winnowed out. On the contrary, these are emphatically public plays, up to their necks in the matter of Ireland. Behind *The Only True History of Lizzie Finn* lies the decline of the Protestant landlord class in Ireland in the late nineteenth century. *The Steward of Christendom* is lit by the flames of Ireland's great conflict between capital and labour, the 1913 Lockout, and the withdrawal of Britain from the South of Ireland in 1922. And *White Woman Street* pivots on the irony of Irish natives, dispossessed on this side of the Atlantic, slaughtering and dispossessing Native Americans on the other side. All three plays are set against a background of recent wars. These are history plays, deeply imbued with the taint of spilt blood. Their beauty arises not from any precious turning away from history, but in spite of an unflinching knowledge of history's horrors.

But the sense of both time and place in these plays is very much that of the late twentieth century. Sebastian Barry writes from a perspective in which both the grand narrative of history and the stability of Ireland as a place are falling apart. The history that informs these plays is a history of counter-currents, of lost strands, of untold stories. Against the simple narrative of Irish history as a long tale of colonisation and resistance, Barry releases more complex stories of people who are, in one way or another, a disgrace to that history. Thomas Dunne and his dead son in *The Steward of Christendom* belong to the long tradition of Irishmen in British uniforms. Robert Gibson in *Lizzie Finn* and Trooper O'Hara in *White Woman Street* are Irishmen who are also veterans of wars of colonisation, not on the side of the natives, but that of the colonisers. These plays are, in that sense, another side of the story.

And if historical time is not simple and stable in the plays, neither is place. The plays are, of course, utterly Irish, but they also acknowledge the terrifying truth that Ireland is not a fixed place. In *Prayers of Sherkin* Fanny Hawke, speaking of Sherkin Island, but touching on an image that serves for the bigger island of Ireland, asks her brother, 'Do you not feel that this island is moored only lightly to the sea-bed, and might be off for the Americas at any moment?' The Ireland of the plays collected here is also moored but lightly to the sea-bed. Lizzie Finn and Robert Gibson trail Ireland, England and Africa behind them, and they belong to a journey rather than a fixed homeland. Lizzie is both a stranger and a native in County Kerry, placed and displaced at the same time. Trooper O'Hara's Ireland is an incongruous Sligo recollected from 'wide America'. And the country in Thomas Dunne's disordered head is a lost land somewhere between London and Dublin, an English Ireland that has disappeared beneath the waves of revolution.

The thread that runs through all of these plays, indeed, is the ambiguity of belonging. The fundamental opposition of Irish history – native on one side, foreigner on the other – is subverted in these figures who defy history by being at the same time both inhabitants and strangers. Lucinda Gibson tells Robert in *Lizzie Finn* that 'people are very simple and they like to know who they are talking to'. But the plays themselves tell us that people are far from simple and that it is impossible to know who you are talking to. Does Lizzie Finn belong in her native Corcaguiney, to which she returns as an exotic stranger? Is Thomas Dunne, proud Irishman and loyal servant of the Crown, a rightful inhabitant of the new State? Is Trooper O'Hara a white warrior or a dark native, a bringer of order or an outlaw?

The answer, or rather the impossibility of answering, is both the curse and the blessing of these people. They are made vulnerable by their own placelessness. Because they cannot be properly defined by the categories in which history moves, they are always in danger of being lost. It is not for nothing that Thomas Dunne, who has lost a kingdom and is now dependent on his three daughters, reminds us of King Lear on the heath as an 'unaccommodated man . . . no more but such a poor bare forked animal'. Stripped of the things that adorn and cover up our bare humanity – nation, place, property – Barry's central characters stand exposed to the cold winds of history.

But that very nakedness is also their salvation. Robert Gibson tells Lizzie Finn that, 'It's only history chooses a person's circumstance . . . We are all very much equal under the clothes that history lends us.' The plays place great weight on this imagery of clothing – Thomas Dunne being measured for his asylum suit, Lizzie Finn's star-spangled stage knickers – but only to draw our attention to the reality of the poor bare forked animal underneath, to the naked equality of embodied humanity. By facing up to the naked vulnerability, Barry is also able to say 'only history', to see history as the borrowed clothing beneath which his people can retain their invulnerable grace.

Because they have no clear, simple historical meaning, the people of the plays are able to escape history's relentless drive to obliterate their memory. Barry's people are the footnotes, the oddities, the quirks of history. The tide of time sweeps them beyond familiar ground, and their part is but to surrender to its implacable swell. In *The Steward of Christendom*, for instance, the central public image is that of the surrender of Dublin Castle to Michael Collins in 1922. The surrender marks the end, not just of Thomas Dunne's public role, but of his meaning for history. The world in which he had a meaning was lost in that moment of surrender. He is fit only for oblivion. Yet, in the end, his disordered mind allows him to remember himself, to call himself to the eye of the mind.

The miracle of each of these plays is that as each piece of human flotsam floats by we see its head still above water, kept buoyant by an invisible ring of words and tenderness. These historically meaningless people come to mean everything to us. In remembering them for us, Sebastian Barry has played to theatre's simplest and most astonishing strength – its power to defy the darkness by lighting up our minds with the unquenchable glow of lost lives.

Fintan O'Toole
May 1995

The Only True History of Lizzie Finn

For Ali

Characters

Lizzie Finn, *mid to late thirties, a strong good-looking person*
Jelly Jane, *robust, handsome, late thirties*
Robert Gibson, *early forties, black hair, a little rough-looking*
Birdy Doyle, *a small pinched man in his forties*
Tilly, *a thin healthy-looking person in her twenties*
Colonel Cody, *a very striking American gentleman*
Bartholomew Grady, *seventies, a plume of white hair*
Lucinda Gibson, *Robert's mother, late sixties, dark like him*
Teresa, *same actor as Tilly but transformed*
Lord Castlemaine, *same actor as Colonel Cody but transformed*
Lady Castlemaine, *same actor as Jelly Jane but transformed*
Factotum, *same actor as Birdy Doyle*
Rector, *same actor as Factotum and Birdy Doyle*
A few **waltzers** *of any description*

The play is set in Weston-super-Mare, Avon, and Inch, Kerry, in the 1890s.

The text of *The Only True History of Lizzie Finn* reproduced here is the script as it went into rehearsal for its first performance at the Abbey Theatre, Dublin, in October 1995.

Act One

Weston-super-Mare, 1890s. Stage left, two chairs, where light makes **Lizzie Finn** *and* **Jelly Jane**'s *dressing room, a nook of soft gaslight.* **Lizzie** *strides on, arriving for her work, starts to take off her day clothes.* **Jelly Jane** *arrives, carrying their stage dresses. They kiss. The low tinkering of the hall beyond.*

Jelly Jane   That old washerwoman would want to watch her work. (*Feeling the dresses.*) They're still damp, Lizzie.

Lizzie   It's the layers. They're hard to get dry. It's the best laundry in Weston-super-Mare. She's a demon with a ribbon iron.

Jelly Jane (*changing*)   I'm that bilious today. I ate two pork pies and now I'm paying twice. I'm like Harry Giles that ate his wife Daisy and was hanged in London last year. They asked him what he wanted for his last breakfast. Stomach powders, he said.

Lizzie (*sitting on a chair in her underthings, gazing at a shoe hanging from its lace*)   That came from King's and Co., the well-known boot and shoe retailer.

Jelly Jane   A girl with a dicky stomach shouldn't high kick for a living.

Lizzie   The salt air's got into it. (*Putting the shoe on.*) It'll look all right in the footlights. Everything does, thank God. (*Her other foot.*) Look at those corns, would you, Jelly Jane? They're worse than my mother's. And she had an excuse for them, wandering the roads of Corcaguiney.

Jelly Jane (*getting into her stage dress*)   The apothecary by the African cenotaph has a yellow balm for them.

Lizzie   An Irish road would kill you.

Jelly Jane   Christ, Lizzie, that Ireland of yours is no good for a holiday anyhow. You're always thinking of your Ireland. I seldom think of my moors.

Lizzie   Since maybe it was you were happy there.

Jelly Jane   Oh, I was. My mother was cushions. (*They face each other, applying each other's white make-up and red lips and cheeks.*) She was too fond of my father though. Fifteen wee'uns, eight living. But she was cushions.

Lizzie   That's our music there now, Jelly Jane.

They pull on their starry knickers, solid garments with gold stars sewn into the crotches to catch the light in the cancan. **Jelly Jane** *half-trips into them.*

Jelly Jane   I'm tired to dance. Man-traps these knickers be, Lizzie.

Before they go onstage they give each other a quick look over.

Lizzie   Shipshape as ships, dear.

Jelly Jane   Yes, yes? Is this old girl presentable? Next year we'll open the shop. What do you say?

Lizzie   Next year. Let us show these provincial boys the style.

They turn smoothly and face out, an arc of limelight falls on them, they're underlit by harsh footlights. They dance the cancan bravely. At the close they throw up their skirts and show their starry knickers. Light only there, the glitter of the gold stars in the darkness. Music.

The yellow whorled light of the beach, a heavy bluster of wind, the spindly shadow of the pier in the distance. Windy music. After a little, **Lizzie** *comes on against the wind, in her good coat, pinning her hat with hatpins.*

Lizzie   All praise to the beggar that invented hatpins. (*Stopping.*) There'll be no little chaps out today, pushing their sailboats through the tide pools.

A man's black hat comes blowing along the sand. She traps it under her foot and lifts it up, and looks in the lining.

(*Reading.*) Robert Godfrey Gibson, Esquire. Now where are you, Robert Godfrey Gibson Esquire that puts your foolish head in here betimes?

Splashing feet. **Robert** *arrives panting, his handsome clothes spattered and speckled with sand and salt water. His hair is a bit wild and black without the hat.*

Robert Success! When a hat gets the wind into it, good Lord. Running along like a blessed dog.

Lizzie (*laughing*) I have it a bit dented after my shoe.

Robert (*taking the offered hat*) It's a Kerry hat, it don't dent easy. Kerry hatters know about storms and dents. (*He gives the inside a determined puck.*) See now? I'll get it brushed and sure it won't know itself.

Lizzie *smiles but now* **Robert** *isn't sure how to proceed. He sets the hat on again and nods and is about to go. Another bluster of wind threatens the hat.* **Lizzie** *laughs and makes a leap at it.*

Lizzie Oh, nearly.

They laugh. **Robert** *puts the hat softly under an arm.*

Robert Best tuck it under my oxter like an army man.

Lizzie Were you in the war that everyone goes to?

Robert I was, with my three brothers. The Transvaal.

Lizzie Everyone goes to the wars these times.

Robert I suppose they do. Thank you for saving my hat, miss.

Lizzie All right, Mr Gibson. (**Robert** *surprised.*) I read it on the lining – before I knew its owner was near.

Robert Oh, that's fine. A hat's not a letter, is it? I thought you knew me. Because, may I ask, before I go, by your way of talking, you are a Kerry person also, are you not?

Lizzie In other days. I don't know what I am now.

Robert No more than myself. (*Makes to go.*)

Lizzie Here. (*Fetching out a hatpin from her own hat.*) Shove that in your hat. You can't go about barehead. You can take it out again when you reach the esplanade. (*Gives him the pin. He laughs loudly, sets his hat on his head and sticks in the pin.*)

Robert *wanders off, laughing still.* **Lizzie** *watches him go.*

Robert (*mostly to himself*)   Thank you, thank you.

Lizzie *sings quietly, staring after him.*

Lizzie   Billy and Maisie and I
Billy and Maisie and I
Try as we try as we try
We can't stop
Because Maisie keeps showing her mop her mop
Because Maisie keeps showing her mop

Robert *comes back as she knew he would.*

Robert   Do you walk here a great deal, Miss?

Lizzie   I walk here only rarely.

Robert   Ah. Rarely. (*Nods and goes obediently.*)

The planky yellow of the music-hall. **Robert** *comes on with a chair and a beer and a playbill, sits himself down, rests the beer on his knee, tries to peruse the bill. Into the limelight steps a little man with a sharp face. He speaks very sadly.* **Robert** *lifts the beer halfway to his lips but the man's voice stills him. He doesn't move again till the end of the turn.*

Birdy Doyle   Good evening to you. My name is Birdy Doyle. I will be doing for you now the Birds of Ohio. (*Pause.*) The Crested Jackhammer. (*Whistles it.*) The Yellow Miner Bird. (*Whistles it.*) The Ohion Sparrow. (*Whistles it.*) The Ohion Spotted Dove. (*Whistles it.*) The American Wood pigeon. (*Calls it.*) The Broken Man. (*Calls it.*) The Red-throated Thrush. (*Whistles it.*) The Lonesome Plover. (*Calls *it.*) That was, The Birds of Ohio. My name is Birdy Doyle. Thank you. (*Goes solemnly.*)

Robert, *the beer still halfway, looks about him, quite taken aback.*

Robert Good Lord.

The music of the cancan. **Robert** *settles in to watch it.* **Lizzie** *and* **Jelly Jane** *come on, begin the dance, with a scattered hoot here and there. It's only after a while that* **Robert** *recognises* **Lizzie**. *He scans the playbill, touches the hatpin briefly that's still in his hat, gets up, puts down the beer messily, starts to peel off his greatcoat, and in a fever rushes the stage, and wraps, or tries to, his coat about* **Lizzie**.

Wait, wait!

Jelly Jane A murderer!

Lizzie What are you doing, mister?

Robert Covering you with this coat.

Lizzie And for why?

Robert You're for better than showing yourself to these broken men.

Lizzie It's my true work. Go away from me in my work!

Robert You needn't show yourself again.

Lizzie You're a stranger. Take your stranger's coat from me.

Jelly Jane Take it from her! (*She strikes him down with great strength.* **Robert** *falls but keeps talking up to* **Lizzie**, *as if falling were nothing to him.*)

Robert What work is it, for a woman that speaks like you?

Lizzie How do I speak? Are you a madman from the asylum up the hill?

Robert No, no, but a man, with a coat.

Jelly Jane *draws* **Lizzie** *away.* **Robert** *stumbles from the stage, coat dragging behind him.*

Lizzie (*shouting after him*)   You shame me, before this hall.
You shame me, you blackguard!

Poor light of the dressing room, **Lizzie** *agitated,* **Jelly Jane** *trying to get her to sit.*

Jelly Jane   Was yon man known to you, Lizzie?

Lizzie   I gave him the time of day, one of my best times of
day, and a hatpin.

Jelly Jane   You gave that man a hatpin?

Lizzie   Yes.

Jelly Jane   But why, my Lizzie?

Lizzie   One of my sixpenny hatpins from the Orient
Bazaar!

Jelly Jane (*shocked*)   In Rhodes Street? (*To herself mostly.*)
She's met him. He'll be one of those false types. To break a
woman's heart – a dancing woman's heart.

Lizzie   Top bill, we are. Names over the sentimental
singers, and the humorous turns. Contract!

Jelly Jane   We are!

Lizzie   I have it all written down, in writing.

Jelly Jane   In bloody writing.

Lizzie   You'll find nowhere just as respectable as theatre
life!

Jelly Jane (*almost jumping at the force of* **Lizzie**)   So I find!

Lizzie (*differently, sitting finally*)   Kerry. Kerry. He's bringing
Kerry in on me.

Jelly Jane   Is that where he's from? The poor man. Maybe
he couldn't help himself so.

Lizzie   Don't be sensible now, Jelly Jane. I don't want to be sensible now. I want to rage and speak nonsense.

Jelly Jane (*sitting close*)   Well now, it's just all you've ever told me about Kerry . . . Will I get something soothing from the corner, pet? Something to still tha hurt? Foreign wine or porter, or Ladies' Gin?

Lizzie (*quietly*)   I want to rage and speak nonsense.

Jelly Jane (*softly*)   Please, please, rage, dear.

Lizzie   I don't like a person to put shame to me. (*After a little.*) My mother went barefoot all her life, but the roads were green all over Corcaguiney then, if there were roads. There used to be a saying about the roads of Corcaguiney, as being things that did not exist. They might say a particular person's virtue was like the roads of Corcaguiney – you know?

Jelly Jane (*listening hard*)   Ah ha.

Lizzie   But in our time there were roads enough, to carry my father and his singing voice about the place. He knew songs from the islands that he didn't sing much, unless we were rowed over to the Blasket on a sweet summer day. He knew tradesmen's songs and tinkers' songs and he knew little parts out of operettas that he could sing for the rich people if he were asked. He liked to sing for the rich because he had a great love of fine chairs and carpets and plates – he liked to look at them in the rooms. But then he'd be as happy to go out on the frosty road again, and be gone, the three of us, be a memory, a memory of singing. And he knew that the people all over Corcaguiney would be humming his tunes about the hills if they wandered there, or about the strands, or in their houses. He was the very singing soul of Corcaguiney. He never let shame be put to us. Singing or dancing to him were the highest things a person could put himself to. And he always said the very heart of a person was revealed in their singing. You could take a dairymaid out of a byre, and set her in the shitty yard, and if she could sing, all paradise and Beulah would appear about her and the listeners would be transported there and then. He took fever from a hungry ditch and my mother followed after him. I will never forget him or dishonour his memory, that singing man. For a man with a singing voice like that is God, or the shadow of God on this earth. And I am the daughter forever of that singing man.

Jelly Jane   You are, Lizzie.

Lizzie   I am.

Bundles of mist unbundling themselves at the edge of the beach, a sense of wetness on the holiday boards, the beach obscured. A neat young woman, **Tilly** *comes on with a folding billboard and sets it in its morning position.* **Robert** *wanders on, trying to see down on to the beach for* **Lizzie**.

Tilly (*nervously*)   Good morning to you, sir.

Robert   Good morning. (*A mite gruffly.*) Misty.

Tilly (*relieved*)   There won't be many on the strand today, sir. Except the regular worm diggers and the gentlemen with the shell nets.

Robert   No – thank God! (*Peering into the mist.*) Is the tide out?

Tilly   Oh, yes, sir. The tide's been like that a long time, since they built the great sea wall at Bristol. Thirty years ago, sir.

Robert   Is that a fact? So what's your name then?

Tilly   Tilly Johns, sir.

Robert   Did you see by any chance, Tilly Johns, a handsome woman, with a green hat maybe, go out upon the strand, walking?

Tilly No, sir. But she may be there for all that. I know the lady you mean.

Robert Oh, you do?

Tilly Lizzie Finn, do you mean, sir, the famous dancer? She's as neat and lovely as a florin, sir. I see her most days.

Robert Oh, do you now?

Tilly She loves the strand. I never had the nerve to speak to her. In the high summer you'll have bands of lads lining the esplanade, watching her go, and I expect longing they knew her.

Robert Is that so now? Bands of them.

Tilly Oh, she's very admired in Weston-super-Mare.

Robert Well. (*He has a good read of the playbill.*) 'Colonel Cody's Wild West Show.' Is that on at the minute?

Tilly It's coming Thursday. It'll be great. They have Indians and everything, and fighting. They'll hold it in the pleasure gardens. Oh, you should go, sir.

Robert I will, I will go. I have a great interest in America. More so than Africa, let me tell you.

Tilly It's tailormade for you then, sir. Buffalo Bill Cody is as much a legend as Lizzie Finn, nearly.

Robert That much? Bless me.

Tilly Well, I've things to do, sir, things to do. It was a great pleasure talking to you, sir. You're kindly.

Robert Oh, thank you. Well. (*She starts to go.*) Goodbye now. (*Looking again at the poster.*) Well, now. Well, now.

Tilly (*stopping up short*) But I forgot, sir!

Robert (*startled*) What?

Tilly I doubt if she'll be here today.

Robert Why so?

Tilly   She was attacked last night in the music-hall. It's all over the town. It was in the *Gazette*. An Irishman, sir, with a great head of black hair and a wild face, and eyes that would burn your heart out of your chest. He sounds like the very devil himself, doesn't he, sir? She'd hardly come down for her walk today.

Robert   But she wasn't injured.

Tilly   I don't know, sir. I hope not. They're looking for the man, to lock the demon up. But I expect he ran for it. He'll be in Dublin now. You've heard of Dublin? It's the big town over there in Ireland.

Robert   I've heard of Dublin.

Tilly (*going*)   There you are now. How did I forget such a thing? It's the mist, must be. (*She goes.* **Robert** *looks about nervously.*)

Low lights of evening, the mist still enduring, coiling about, drifting across a sign at the back of the music-hall, that reads STAGE.
Robert *comes on with a fist of red roses that are melting in the mist, the petals dropping, much to his concern.*

Robert   I'm bringing stalks to her, stalks. That won't help me.

Lizzie *comes to the sign, looks out, examining the weather, pulling on yellow gloves, and sees* **Robert**. *She stills.*

Lizzie Finn, Lizzie Finn, is that you?

Lizzie   Who wants to know? I have fine big strong men inside to call to if I need.

Robert   It's myself, and I am most dreadfully sorry to have assaulted you last night with my coat. It wasn't till I heard that the authorities were looking for me that I understood

the full horror of what I had done. Now I'm in fear of them
taking me away before I can apologise to you.

Lizzie So you should be. (*Quietly.*) You blackguard.

Robert Indeed and I am, and I've brought you these . . .
(*Looking at the ruined flowers.*) These sorry, sorry blooms . . .
The mist has dissolved them and loosened these red sparks
on to the lane . . .

Lizzie You'd better take that out of your hat.

Robert Take what?

Lizzie That, what I gave you.

Robert (*touching it*) The hatpin? I'd forgotten all about it.

Lizzie Well, I told them you might be wearing one. They
gave each other very queer looks about it, I can tell you.

Robert (*taking it out*) I've never been sought by the police
before . . .

Lizzie Oh, it's not only the police.

Robert Who else?

Lizzie The asylum men. They want you up there on the
hill to teach you your manners. They've a nice white jacket
for you in place of your coat.

Robert If you could understand why I did it . . .

Lizzie I don't need to, do I? Jelly Jane is the chief witness
but you were considerate enough to attack me in front of a
hundred of my most devoted followers, the Monday night
crowd itself.

Robert No, you don't need to. I should submit to them
really. You've no idea how tired I am. I haven't slept for
months.

Lizzie Well, you'll get a good sleep maybe up the hill, if
they catch you.

Robert I suppose so. (*Breaks down.*)

After a little, **Lizzie** *comes down to him bravely.*

Lizzie   What is it then, Mr Gibson, that has you so trigger-happy with your coat in music-halls?

Robert   Bless me, I don't think I can say now, after breaking down so. Oh, it's a foolish world. Full of foolishness and foolish actions. Don't you think?

Lizzie   You better tell me, or I'll call to my cohorts within.

Robert   It was Africa, Lizzie Finn. Africa. I'm half a year coming home like a lame dog cut up in the hunt. I've no heart for staying and no heart for going. I'd rather be a spirit, you know, a little puff of a what-do-they-call-it, a ghost. It was Africa. I buried my three brothers there.

Lizzie (*after a little*)   Here, I'll take your nice roses, Mr Gibson. (*She does.*)

Robert   Thank you.

Lizzie   Will you meet me again, in the daylight?

Robert   Oh, yes. Oh, yes, Miss Finn.

Lizzie   Off you go. You'll sleep tonight. Go on. (*He does.*) Is all the wars in the world worth these broken gentlemen?

A simple nest of linen bolstered by feathers. A dim light is thrown up from the foot of the bed, by a meagre summer fire. **Lizzie** *and* **Jelly Jane** *lit snug in the mass of white linen,* **Jelly Jane** *with a fierce nightcap,* **Lizzie***'s famous hair spread down a pillow. They have their arms out, still and straight before them on their stomachs. All the rest of the stage in pleasant darkness.*

Lizzie   He's a very strange man, Jelly Jane.

Jelly Jane   Do you think you should meet a man like that? Maybe, do you know, he has a little silver knife he likes to stick into ladies, like the Manchester Prowler. Or maybe, do

you know, a taste for you, boiled in a big pot, like poor
Harry Giles that was.

Lizzie   No, he's just a big sad sort of a fella.

Jelly Jane   I suppose he's just a wanderer coming through
Weston-super-Mare like many another. (**Lizzie** *acknowledges
this.*) I suppose he's as much flotsam and jetsam as a
thousand others you'd see in the halls of England? (**Lizzie**
acknowledges this.) I suppose as women we go for the ones that
we go for and no explanations. (**Lizzie** *acknowledges this.*) I
suppose that's how it happens.

Lizzie   I suppose, Jelly Jane.

Jelly Jane   Well, it's very mysterious and a girl would do as
well to be philosophic about it, as aught else.

Lizzie   Oh, yes.

*Across the stage from them slowly a crescent moon appears small and
high, and then the intermittent thrown light of a lighthouse.* **Robert**
*stands in the dark alone, it's somewhere high above the town, and
solitary, with a fall to the sounding sea below, and a stirring cliff
breeze against him. He's gazing down.*

Jelly Jane (*holding one of* **Lizzie**'s *hands across the linen*)   I'll
say the one thing, dear, and then hold my whist, as you'd
say. (**Lizzie** *looks at her peacefully.*) I do hope he's not like the
roads of Corcaguiney. (**Lizzie** *lays her head in against* **Jelly
Jane**'s.)

Lizzie   What can you do, dear?

Jelly Jane (*staring forward into the firelight*)   Not much, is the
answer to that, Lizzie. Not much.

Robert (*makes to jump but doesn't*)   If I were Isambard
Kingdom Brunel I'd throw a bridge from here to Wales.

*He raises his arms up. The light from the lighthouse washes across
him. He laughs in his privacy.*

I would, I would!

The many-coloured bunting of the pleasure gardens a week later, the colours flying, a rail upstage to protect the spectators, beyond which Colonel Cody and his Show will take place. **Robert** *in highly polished shoes and* **Lizzie** *in her summer finery stroll on, accompanied by* **Jelly Jane**, *looking a little awkward.*

Jelly Jane   It's a wonder, I'm told, by ones who were here last week. The American Waggoners get put upon by Savage Redmen and the Colonel saves them with his Horsemen. Well, you wouldn't think grown people would pay four shillings for that, on a lovely summer's afternoon, when they could be away at the bathing huts for naught and be putting sand in their knickers. And I never did like shepherding folk.

Lizzie   Chaperoning, is what you're doing, girl, not shepherding, and I am very grateful to you for it, as you know.

Jelly Jane (*mostly to herself*)   Shepherding's more like it, with that big black sheep beside you. There's it starting up now. They're fierce-looking chaps, them Redmen, all the same. It's all miles off, I can't see a thing. (*She ducks under the rail and disappears off.*)

A clatter of gunfire and whoops of the Indians and an explosion of spectacle.

Lizzie (*grabbing* **Robert**'*s arm*)   They're blasting them, they're blasting them!

Robert (*laughing*)   But they'll be fine just after!

Lizzie   But see that blood, that drenching of blood! And the terrible fire from the guns of the outlaws!

Robert   Settlers, Lizzie. Don't you want the Settlers to win America?

Lizzie   I do not, I do not! Hurrah the Redmen, hurrah the Redmen!

A pause as they watch something.

Robert   Is that our chaperone?

Lizzie (*hands up to her cheeks*)   Oh my good Lord! Oh, my Lord! Oh, Jelly Jane!

Robert   Christ, he rode right across her. Stay here, Lizzie, I'll go out there and fetch her! (*He ducks under the rail and rushes off.*)

Lizzie   Oh, oh, oh, oh, oh.

Robert *struggles back carrying an indignant* **Jelly Jane**.

Is she all right, Robert?

Jelly Jane   Would you . . . I'm not hurt, you fool. Put me down.

Robert (*laying her on the ground gently*)   She's hurt her leg, Lizzie, don't mind her.

Jelly Jane   Look, he's after me now.

Robert (*raising her skirt*)   You're all right, Miss Jane, you're all right. I was a soldier. I know a wound like this. Let me assist you, won't you.

Jelly Jane   Are you so sure you know tha way about my legs?

Robert   I do. (*He rips part of her drawers.* **Jelly Jane** *screams.*)

Jelly Jane   What sort of doctoring is that? I paid seven shillings for those Belgian drawers.

Lizzie   Hush a moment, he has to bind you, I think.

Colonel Cody *in all his moustached splendour comes out to them. He's quite elderly but very striking in his working outfit. There's a few moments of silence as* **Jelly Jane** *takes him in.* **Robert** *instinctively rises from* **Jelly Jane**, **Colonel Cody** *takes his place.*

Cody   A thousand abject apologies, my dear. I do believe you caught a blow of a hoof on your lovely leg. (*He examines it.*)

Jelly Jane   You don't have to mind if you touch my leg a little.

Cody Why, think of me as a medical man, for the moment, my dear.

Jelly Jane Oh, yes.

Just the spectacle of them for a while, **Robert** *and* **Lizzie** *looking down at* **Jelly Jane**, **Jelly Jane** *looking into* **Colonel Cody**'s *face.*

Oh, Lizzie. Oh. (*Dizzy.*) Now I feel it. Oh. (*Blacks out.*)

Towards evening, on the spot where **Robert** *stood in the darkness.* **Lizzie** *and* **Robert** *face each other, their hands held forward and joined.*

Robert Look at that trawler below, so far, so clear, like an almond on the sea. I was up here just a week ago, the night I brought you the roses, there was just a bit of a moon and the lighthouse on the point washing its light on me now and then.

Lizzie That's a lonely life. I hope he gets into the hall betimes, so he can see what fun is.

Robert Who, Lizzie?

Lizzie The lighthouse keeper.

Robert Of course, yes. Lizzie, I would like to take you home with me, if you'll come. I don't think I'd care very much to go now without you.

Lizzie Won't you stay and be my Robert here and watch me dance in England? It's not so easy to dance in Ireland.

Robert Lizzie, if you give me your kiss, it may be easy enough.

Lizzie You can take my kiss. Here, take it.

They kiss.

Robert (*close to her*) I took your kiss.

Lizzie You took it. And when they blame me for it I'll tell them to the last you took it. But I think they won't believe me.

A convivial gathering backstage, in farewell to **Lizzie** *and* **Robert**. **Jelly Jane** *in a chair with her wounded leg up,* **Colonel Cody** *attending her assiduously.* **Birdy Doyle** *rather alone on a chair.* **Lizzie** *standing, aglow, and* **Robert** *pouring out a fine red liquid into* **Jelly Jane**'s *glass.*

Birdy Doyle We must drink a fond farewell.

Robert I hope your lovely leg heals quickly, Jelly Jane, and you'll be back dancing for the autumn season.

Jelly Jane Oh, mercy, Robert Gibson, I'll dance no more if my present luck holds out, and the Colonel will give me a job as a Western Waggoner, he says.

Cody And so I shall!

Jelly Jane I'm to be overwhelmed by Redmen every day of the week, Lizzie. Come here to me, girl, so we can whisper. (**Lizzie** *kneels in to her.*) That we lived so long, Lizzie, to witness these miracles that stun our hearts.

Birdy Doyle We must drink a fond farewell!

Jelly Jane And so we must. A farewell to music-halls and maidenhood, perhaps, if I prove a decent Western Waggoner in the upshot. Here's to Lizzie and her Robert and their Ireland, and may they prosper there as they deserve. Seven years Lizzie and I did show our legs to the English lads, and they have been the dearest and the fondest days of my life!

Lizzie Oh, Jelly Jane.

They all drink.

Jelly Jane We're going to have to have singing now, or

we're not worth our salt. For if you can't sing when you're sad you can't sing when you're happy.

Birdy Doyle   We must drink a fond farewell!

Jelly Jane   We've done that now, Birdy. Now Robert Gibson, a soldier always has songs, come on now, as bawdy as you like.

Robert   I think I only have hymns. I don't think hymns is what we want just now.

Lizzie   Oh, Robert, only hymns? I'll have to be teaching you good wicked songs.

Jelly Jane   All right then, Lizzie, girl, a wicked song. Let his education begin tonight!

Lizzie *fits herself to sing. She does the full act on it, striding and smiling, putting it over. It's true that her voice is poor enough, but it doesn't hinder her.*

Lizzie   I never knew a man that didn't like lemon
that didn't like a lemon in his tea
I never knew a man that didn't like singing
if he's singing to my doh-ray-me

     Spoken chorus: What's she on about?

I never knew a man that didn't like kisses
that didn't like some kisses now and then
I never knew a man that didn't go a-hunting
a-hunting for my sweet little wren

     Chorus.

I never knew a man that didn't care for dancing
dancing with the ladies of the town
Oh but I never knew a man that didn't like sitting
Sitting on my sweet Fanny Brown

     Chorus.

General laughter and raising of glasses.

Well, Colonel, I hope you'll favour us with a song. It's
always a privilege to hear a foreign song.

Cody   Well, ladies and gentlemen, I'm not noted for the
beauty of my voice, it's true. But if you'll bear with me, I'll
sing you a song that a man in Wyoming wrote for me
especial, in the old gone days of my youth.

> I went out to shoot the buffalo
> with my gun so bright
> I saw them moving like the sea
> in the dying light
>
> > *Chorus:*
> > I saw them moving like the sea
> > as I let my pony rest
> > I was thinking to myself right then
> > I love this West the best
>
> The hills were high and ranged about
> the river was like gold
> a man could live here all his life
> and never would grow old
>
> > *Chorus.*
>
> But days they come and days they go
> and changes are our lot
> and I travel now no more, my friends,
> in the Land that Time Forgot
>
> > *Chorus.*

A bit of a silence. **Jelly Jane** *touches* **Colonel Cody**'s *arm.*

Birdy Doyle   We must bid a fond farewell.

The stage of the music-hall in the late night. **Lizzie** *alone in the
dimness, looking out over the empty hall. She gives a half-swish to the*

front of her day dress, as if her dance was running through her head. Out of the shadows comes **Jelly Jane**, *hobbling along on her stick.*

Jelly Jane   Look at me, Lizzie. A far cry.

Lizzie *smiles at her.*

Lizzie   Well, girl, to give it all up, it isn't easy after all.

Jelly Jane   Ah, girl, it's high time. We're getting so long in the tooth we'd have to start putting more comedy into the dancing, because they like to see young legs when they look at legs.

Lizzie   I suppose so. But you are the one dearest to me besides Robert. You must come and see us in Ireland.

Jelly Jane (*not believing it*) Oh, yes.

Lizzie   I know I'm supposed to be brave Lizzie Finn, but, I tell you, girl, I'm half-afraid to go.

Jelly Jane   Think of the grandeur of it, Lizzie. The train will take you away through the Welsh farms, there'll be lamps across the fields in the dark towns, and you'll sit knee to knee with him. Don't be afraid ever to go back to your own people.

Lizzie   Oh, Jelly Jane, Jelly Jane. I'll miss all this. I was warm in our bed.

Jelly Jane   Ah, girl. Here, I wanted to give you this. (*Handing her a little stone figure.*)

Lizzie   What is it, Jelly Jane?

Jelly Jane   It's a little stone angel, you see. My father dug it up one time in his field. Some say it was in there from the time of the giants, I don't know. He gave it to me when I was going south and I'm giving it to you now.

Lizzie   I can't take your father's gift.

Jelly Jane   Something to watch over you, Lizzie. (*Closing her hands around hers with the figure in them.*) Something of Yorkshire, where you've never been. Something of Jelly Jane.

Lizzie   She's beautiful.

Jelly Jane   You can give it to any child of yours if you wish. Let it protect you and yours and bring you safely through whatever troubles there must be.

Lizzie   These have been very strange and unexpected days.

Jelly Jane   Love always comes mysteriously, girl. Didn't we know that? I'll leave you in peace and bid you goodnight.

Lizzie   I'm very honoured by your gift, and by your friendship.

Jelly Jane (*winking*)   Likewise, likewise, Lizzie Finn. (*Going, then stopping, looking back.*) You're the dandiest girl a girl could know, Lizzie Finn.

Above Inch Strand in Kerry. Right, a structure suggesting the old house tower, a sort of lumber room, where rest bits of lawn sports, trophies from wars and old items, old dolls, a basin to catch a quiet drip, the newest thing being three army uniforms on a rough rack, all in a dusty solitude, with a few wooden steps leading up to it. Left, the comfortable sitting area of a drawing room, appropriate to a small gentleman's house, good chairs and a richly embroidered sofa, and a little elegant table for a lamp and a vase. There's a little pair of reading glasses on this table. Downstage, the garden leading off from the drawing room, a roll of trim lawn, with a deal of rhododendron, fuschia and peony, and roses. A simple well and a bucket. An open enough feeling, but also the sense of shelter from the high wilderness beyond the house. The garden thick with birds, the fresh pounding of the sea in Dingle Bay below, running in on to Inch Strand. A fresh, hot high summer's day towards late afternoon. Now through the pulse of sun comes **Bartholomew Grady,** *the gardener, a stocky man of about seventy with a fire of white hair still. He carries a basket lined with wet dock leaves which he will put cut roses into for moistness. He waves his old cutting knife, a contraption tied about with ancient string, at the retinue of black flies above his head.*

Bartholomew   Can not a Christian gardener cross his lawn without assassins? All winter, wrapped by my fire, I think of you sleeping in the icy stones, waiting for these sprightly summer days. (*He manages, however, to select a few blooms, expertly snipping them into his basket.*)

Lucinda Gibson, *Robert's mother, tall, dark, with a plain silver cross on the breast of her brocaded black mourning dress, comes through the drawing room with a rectangle of paper, looking for good light to read it by. She steps out into the garden, closely scanning the paper.*

Lady, now, don't come out here without your netted hat – these black men will divide in the air, like demons, and ambush you too.

Lucinda   A little rough boy has just come running along the sea road from Castlemaine with a telegraph message. I'm sure his father sent him, with all the haste that is due to a telegraph message. And, look, I can't read it at all, Bartholomew. It is smudged of course.

Bartholomew   I've the responsibility of these blooms, lady. You know how the heat runs in under the dock leaves. I can't be scanning over messages at the same time. You'd best be burning a thing like that, lady – that's my counsel.

Lucinda   Of your charity, Bartholomew Grady. (*She gives him the telegram.*)

Bartholomew   Fortunate for you I've still immaculate sight. Here, hold it for me again, please, lady. (*He hands her the telegram back and she holds it unfolded for him. He steps back a few paces.*) By Napoleon's ghost, I can read anything, at four paces. There now. All nicely read now. (*Heading off.*)

Lucinda   But what does it say, Bartholomew? Is it good or bad?

Bartholomew   I don't know if it's good or bad. It will be as well for me to say nothing, lady. (*He heads off, stooping at the bucket briefly to skite a handful of moisture on to his selections.*)

Lucinda   I'll fetch on my reading glasses. (*She goes to the little table where her glasses are, examines the paper.*) That old man doesn't get any saner. (*Reads.*) What could this be? Bartholomew?

Bartholomew (*just about to escape*) Yes, lady?

Lucinda (*coming back out*) Was there anything in your newspaper about Robert?

Bartholomew No, lady.

Lucinda Nothing at all?

Bartholomew The *Castlemaine Herald* confines itself mostly to the state of the country and the frequent occurrence of murder in Irish life.

Lucinda You spotted nothing throughout the newspaper that would cast light on this telegraph message?

Bartholomew Believe me, lady, I combed it through as is my custom when I am ingesting my sausages at noon and, *mirabile dictu*, as Virgil often said, there wasn't a blessed thing about your son.

Lucinda (*ignoring his sarcasm*) Then it's a mistake. (*Stuffing the message away.*) It has been taken down wrongly at the post office. Honoria Fanning is half-deaf as we all know and her husband is half-blind. The perfect people to run a post office. (*She goes back into the house.*)

Bartholomew Half-blind, says she.

The sky above is reddening into long streaks, with lines of gold. The birds are hushed. He looks at the well.

A well is a kind of unturned bell, that will ring neither matins nor evensong. Ah, yes. (*Goes.*)

The sky deepens to the slate and crimson of late sunset, the dark filling slowly. Upstage, on a high trap, with the strike of the pony's trotting hooves, **Robert** *and* **Lizzie***, with a chequered rug across their legs against the night.*

Robert (*exhilarated*)   Glorious, oh, glorious, my lovely Kerry. Three years, Lizzie.

Lizzie   Those are woods, aren't they, on the headland? I don't ever recall woods in Kerry. Isn't that strange?

Robert   They're my woods, Lizzie. Your woods. Our woods. See the lovely swagger of Inch Strand, Lizzie. That's your strand now.

Lizzie   It's white as a snow bear that I saw once in a menagerie.

Robert   It's famous all over for its beauty. I was happy there often with my brothers. That was our Africa once. And now we'll fill it again with brothers and sisters!

Lizzie   It's handsome, Robert.

Robert   There's the house peeking through the trees – Bartholomew's windbreakers, they are, to protect his garden. I've missed his bitter tongue. Oh, I'm so proud to be bringing you here, Lizzie.

Lizzie   I don't see the house you mean. That little place there by the strand?

Robert   Lizzie, that's the village, as we call it. There was an old body there that gathered the periwinkles.

Lizzie   Not those big roofs and the dark tower?

Robert   That's your home.

Lizzie   But, Robert, that's a landlord's house, isn't it?

Robert   Well, and if it is? What did you think you were coming to?

Lizzie   Not a great place like that, dark against the incoming night.

Robert   It's not so great, believe me. Just a little place, Lizzie. Just a little place for the Gibsons to lay their heads. Are you so shy of it? Will we rest up another night in the hotel in Castlemaine?

Lizzie   I might have been happier approaching in daylight. Twilight is so full of things past. But since we're this far, let's drive on. I can imagine the three of us, my father and mother and me, on this road.

Robert   Remember, Lizzie, you're my wife. You're strong and right and legal here.

Lizzie   Oh, I'm not afraid.

Robert   There's nothing to fear.

Lizzie   Go on away up so.

A deep light in the drawing room, brown shadows shoaling between the chairs. **Teresa**, *the general servant, a birdlike young woman of twenty, comes in, with Bartholomew's roses carefully in her arms. She sets them down gently and digs in her pocket for a Lucifer, strikes it, removes the glass of the lamp, lights it. The room shrugs in the blowing light till she replaces the glass. She arranges the roses in the vase intently, casting shadows everywhere. At the other side of the house, the iron clanging of the bell. She hurries excitedly from the room. Echoing phrases, bang of things, silence for a little, then* **Teresa** *reappears showing* **Lizzie** *into the drawing room.*

Teresa (*breathless*)   You go in there, do, miss, there's a heap of nice places for sitting. (*Watching* **Lizzie** *all the while.*) Would you like your coat off, missy? (*She takes* **Lizzie**'s *coat, lays it on her arm, stroking the material. She takes* **Lizzie**'s *hat in further wonder.*) I never seen an English lady before, missy. You do look lovely if I may say. Are everyone in England so trim? I imagine so, missy.

Lizzie   England has its style, that's true, girl. But that's a nice frock you're wearing yourself.

Teresa (*overcome*)   This old thing, missy? It's only a yard of dross material the mistress bought for me in Tralee.

Lizzie   Well, it's not the dress but the girl in the dress, we used to say.

Teresa   Oh, missy. You've no notion of the excitement you've caused me. Barty has been sputtering by the stoves with all sorts of black words, poking at the ashes with his pruning knife and doing it no good, but I couldn't get my rest last night for thinking of you. Oh, don't mind my give-out, missy. I'm worse than a goose. (*Going, then worriedly.*) You know what a goose is?

Lizzie   I do.

Teresa   Ah, geese are all over. I knew that! (*Goes.*)

Lizzie *left alone. She looks about for a mirror or something to see herself in, attends to her hair.*

Lizzie   I didn't know he was a king, I didn't know. (*She sits ill at ease on a chair, looks at the fireplace.*) He'd be set there on a hearth like that, singing. My father. Lovely Neapolitan songs to break your heart. He'd be given a pair of hard shoes to stand in, so as not to cause offence. Then they'd take them off him at the door. And off into the night with us with our sixpence. Oh, Lord.

A while later, **Robert** *sitting beside* **Lizzie**, *and* **Lucinda** *facing them. There's a certain strain in the room.* **Teresa** *arrives with tea-things on a tray.*

Lucinda   Well done, Teresa, well done. Set it down there. Good girl. (*Smiling out to* **Robert** *and* **Lizzie**.) Yes. Will you do the salmon for the travellers' supper?

Teresa   Oh, it's well on now, lady, well on.

Lucinda Poached, I trust, Teresa? I can't abide salmon, really, unless someone poaches it.

Lizzie You mean stolen?

Teresa No, no, missy – broiled. It is, lady – just as you told me.

Lucinda Thank God. (*She pours the tea with* **Teresa**'s *help.* **Teresa** *hands out the cups.*) That's the girl. She has trained up beautifully, hasn't she?

Teresa Will I bring in candles, lady? Now that there's more folk than one?

Lucinda Do we need candles?

Robert There's light enough.

Lucinda The light of candles draws us in from outdoors, I always think. Draws our hearts within the house. The countryside lies about us, but the candles draw us away from it. Usher in our souls, as it were. A lamp doesn't have the same effect somehow.

Lizzie You like the garden and the countryside?

Lucinda I could stand all evening in the garden listening to the bay running in on Inch, I could. Do you like the tea?

Lizzie Yes, I do, Mrs Gibson.

Lucinda Oh, Lady Gibson, it is. My husband was knighted for his jurisprudence hereabout, but, Lord knows, they flattered him.

Lizzie Excuse me – I didn't know.

Lucinda At any rate, you're Mrs Gibson now, so there won't be too much confusion between us. (*Seeing that* **Teresa** *hasn't moved for a while.*) What's amiss, Teresa, are you all right?

Teresa I have a scream coming on, lady, you must forgive me. I got a terrible cold feeling in my bones when you spoke of souls and suchlike.

Lucinda   Well, don't scream in here, please. You go and scream in peace in the kitchens. When you get a chance, you may unpack their suitcases and portmanteaus.

Teresa   Yes, lady.

Lucinda   We'll manage here.

Teresa   Yes, lady. Thank you, lady. (*She goes.*)

Robert   Still mad as a March hare.

Lucinda   But very malleable, very. I'm quite pleased with her. (*To* **Lizzie**.) Of course, she'll be yours now to perfect.

Lizzie   I don't understand you, Lady Gibson.

Lucinda   This is Robert's house, you know. You've married him, and you must be mistress. Of course, if you wish, I can go to my people in Yorkshire.

Lizzie   Oh, Yorkshire.

Robert   Your people in Yorkshire are underground these many years. There's no question of you being ousted in any way.

Lucinda   Oh, dear me, ousted, no. Thank you, Robert. The plain fact is, dear, since the government transferred the bulk of our farms, it has proved quite difficult to keep things going. Since our whole economy was based on rents.

Robert   I mean to look into all that. I'm sure we can manage for the three of us.

Lucinda   So many in recent years have had to leave their efforts here and go. It's quite sad, really.

Robert   We have a touch of new capital now.

Lucinda (*looking at* **Lizzie**)   Oh, have we? How nice. Where are your people from, Mrs Gibson?

Lizzie   My mother was from Ventry and my father I believe from somewhere near Caherconree, but they moved about Corcaguiney.

Lucinda   They moved about?

Lizzie He travelled from place to place with us.

Lucinda And did he have property here?

Lizzie He had a wife and a child and a splendid singing voice.

Lucinda You mean your father moved about, singing?

Lizzie Yes.

Lucinda How unusual, Robert. And they are both deceased, sadly, your parents?

Lizzie Yes, Lady Gibson. They died of fever.

Lucinda So much death. Robert, after giving me an account of his brothers, tells me you were married in the Presbyterian church in Rutland Square. Does he mean you are a Presbyterian rather than of the Established Church?

Lizzie Yes, of course.

Lucinda I don't want you to think me bigoted, you see. I just wished to know. It's the kind of thing one likes to know about one's daughter-in-law. If you have a little fortune, dear, how did it come to be?

Lizzie I gathered it for myself over the years.

Lucinda How very extraordinary. How did you do that remarkable thing?

Lizzie You don't follow the halls, I think.

Lucinda The halls?

Lizzie The music-halls.

Lucinda Oh, no, dear. Do you?

Robert Lizzie is a very independent woman, Mamma, and has lived an independent life, for which she is to be admired. She suffered here in Corcaguiney as a young girl, and I think it is wrong of you to question her like this, if I may say so.

Lucinda   Well, Robert, you know I have the highest regard for you, and I understand how dreadful it has been for you out there in Africa, and indeed I feel the force of our tragedy just as horribly as I know you do, but this is the plain world out here in Kerry, and the people hereabouts will want to know about your wife before they bring her into their houses. That's just how things are. I know these are modern times, and we are surely heading into darker times yet, but people are very simple and they like to know who they are talking to. That's all.

Robert   I should think they must be proud to know Lizzie.

Lucinda   My dear, these are very ordinary people out here. They expect a marriage in Christ Church like all your family before you. They want to read about her trousseau in the *Irish Times* and they want to feel that their world is going on at least as it always has gone on. You can't expect any better of them, especially in these hard times. I hope you won't disregard that. Because I myself feel quite put out, even to a degree, put upon, by this, I'm sorry to say.

Robert   I don't know why you would be, Mamma.

Lucinda   Well, I've tried to explain to you as gently as I can. I can see you have fine qualities, Mrs Gibson, but you mustn't expect to thrive here immediately. Go about with some care for people's foolish expectations. If you wish to gain your ground eventually. You are very different to the run of girls we get around here.

Lizzie   I expect so.

Lucinda (*rising*)   Now, if you wish me to, I'll see to dinner. I'm sure you're both famished. In a private sense, I bid you welcome to Red House. In other senses, I don't know how I will enjoy describing you to people, but be that as it may.

Robert   You needn't try, Mamma, believe me.

Lucinda   We shall see, my dear.

A few minutes later. **Robert** *kneels before* **Lizzie**, *holding her because she's upset.*

Robert It's only history chooses a person's circumstance.

Lizzie Partly I love you because you don't care about all that.

Robert That's it. I admire you, Lizzie. You didn't lie down and die in Corcaguiney. We are all very much equal under the clothes that history lends us. If you can sing or dance or go soldiering, so much the better for you. No one knows exactly the through-going of their days. You made yourself secure in England. You don't require telling whether it was well or ill done.

Lizzie It was better than many of the doings of Corcaguiney, let me tell you, Robert. How it comes back to me, sitting under these dark skies.

Robert You are the finest person I've ever met, and I've met my share of fine people, in the army and generally.

Lizzie Shall I go up and help little Teresa to unpack our things? She's a nice little creature, I think.

Robert We'll both go up. We'll put on our finery and have a lovely supper of Corcaguiney salmon and the devil take the lingerer.

Lizzie You haven't let me down, sweet.

Robert Nor will I ever, Lizzie.

They go.

The house as if empty, the little ruckus of moonlight through it and the fresh falling of the sea below. A rising and falling music. After a little, **Teresa** *emerges, staggering under the weight of some empty cases. She climbs the steps to the house tower, and lets the cases drop.* **Lizzie***'s stage knickers fall out of one of them.*

Teresa   My, what dust! I'll ignore it. For I can't bide long near these poor uniforms. Three such lovely boys, and naught left of them but this tired cloth, by God. (*Sensing a scream coming on.*) Ah, I won't scream, because they are poor killed lads now. (*To the uniforms.*) I might offend ye. (*Attending the cases.*) That new missis is full of style. She has dresses! (*She spots the knickers, takes them up, examines them in some wonder.*) Ho, there's style for you. Will you take a gander at them stars. Would you deck them? (*Holds the knickers against herself. They seem enormous.*) Ha, ha. Oh. They must be winter knickers. The heaviness of them. Now I've seen the heaven of knickers. She must have been a empress before Robert Gibson found her. Oh, the Holy Christ, that'll keep me going till Christmas. I needs see nothing else till then. (*Holding them aloft.*) Oh, what knickers!

Curtain.

Act Two

The reverse side of the house, represented by, left, broad granite steps up to the open hall. A sense of pillars. It's late September, and there's a big fire in the marble hearth, a bracket of unlit candles on a wall. Twilight infects the piece of gravel before the steps. But mostly, right and downstage, there's a broad bare area, for the strand, and a tufted dune upstage right, and a sense of an old shell midden there. A cold-looking moon has arisen. There's a heap of tangled greenery piled left, Bartholomew's, with a pitchfork stuck into it. A strong sense of the slightly agitated night tide, and of frost. **Teresa** *comes across the hall bearing logs, drops them with a clatter on to the hearth, and carefully places some on to the fire. She takes a long taper from her waistband and lights it in the fire, takes it to the candles, sets a chair under them, and lights them with some effort. The pleasing light grows in the hall. Now* **Bartholomew** *drags on further debris on a big cloth, bringing it to the heap, groaning as he straightens again.* **Teresa** *comes to the top of the steps.*

Teresa Do you not feel that chill on you, Barty? Of course, my poor mother will say this is winter. Her summer is the first week of June, when she gets her journey home to us, for the few holy days given her by Lady Castlemaine. The rest of the year is winter. By her calendar. Isn't that strange? But September is maybe winter, is it, Barty?

Bartholomew It is for various growing things, I don't know about your mother.

Teresa Ah, she was hired to a farmer up beyond Mary's Mountain when she was but five years old. She was a little slave to work. Which is the why she takes such a bleak view of the seasons, I'm sure. And the poor girl fifty-five now. Barty?

Bartholomew (*hoisting some of the garden refuse on to the heap with the pitchfork*) Yes, doty?

Teresa Barty, dear, what do you say about the new missis, now we've had a while to know her?

Bartholomew (*resting*) Well, doty – fact is – she will never do.

Teresa Oh, but you see her clothes, Barty. The solidest style of clothes I ever saw. It does my soul good to watch them.

Bartholomew Clothes are very well.

Teresa I depend on you for wisdom, Barty. I'm disappointed at you. (*Going in again.*) Her clothes speak well for her. (*Coming back a moment, indignant.*) If I ever had such attire, I'd expect you to think well of me.

Bartholomew (*surprised*) And I would, surely.

Teresa *goes in having made her point.* **Bartholomew**, *shaking his head, starts to fix an old pipe for himself, in the growing dark. At length* **Robert** *comes on wearing an old working coat and a battered hat. He has a sack of tools.* **Bartholomew** *spies the figure, extracts the pitchfork, and with force brandishes the pitchfork at him, not seeing who it is.*

What do you do there? Clear off. I'm not afraid, mind.

Robert Is that how you talk to beggars?

Bartholomew It's how I talk to thieves! I'll put this in your ragged coat for you! Go back away!

Robert (*holding up the bag to protect himself*) I heard you were a fierce old warrior.

Bartholomew I'll give you old, I'll give you old, you blackguard! (*Starts to rush at him with the pitchfork.*)

Robert (*shoving the bag into the way of the fork*) Heavens, I'm only playing a game with you, don't kill me. (*Raising his hat.*)

Bartholomew (*halted*) Oh, Mr Robert. Forgive me, do. Why couldn't you say your name in the dark?

Robert You hardly gave me a chance, Bartholomew.

Bartholomew You weren't on the public road dressed like that?

Robert   I was mending fences down at the river. The flood tore some posts out. I was expecting two fellows to help me but they didn't come. So I saw to it myself.

Bartholomew   They wouldn't come to you? Would you credit that? That's for because they think they're all kings now, with the new laws – kings of thistles and rushes.

Robert   Well, kings can linger by their fires, if they wish. Isn't it for the better, Bartholomew?

Bartholomew   No, is the short answer.

Robert (*going up the steps*) This is a lovely night now. Look at the strand. I feel better for the labour. I thought you were going to kill me for certain, Bartholomew, with your nice pitchfork. (*Goes in across the hall.*)

Movement and clatter in the hall now as **Robert**, *come back again, draws chairs up to the hall fire for the evening.* **Lizzie** *comes on carrying a folded cloth on her arm, with* **Teresa** *worriedly beside her.*

Teresa   But that's old Ventry linen, missy, you wouldn't want to go cutting that up – would you? It's fine stuff off the beds.

Lizzie   Well, girl, if it makes a fine sheet won't it make a fine dress? You'll have a fine dress made of old Ventry linen, and you can say it to who you like, can't she, Robert?

Robert (*into the fire, with a book*)   I should think so.

Lizzie   It will be honoured more as a dress than a sheet, girl.

Teresa   Well, if you say.

Lizzie   I have pieces of silk we can sew on to it in plaquettes. And I have gold ribbon too. You'll have a lovely dress for your November dances. Now, stand, while I measure you.

Lizzie *takes out a long tape and a piece of paper, and begins to take measurements of* **Teresa**, *noting them down as she goes.*

What a perfect little person you are, Teresa. Everything matching up like a goddess.

Teresa   Oh, jackanapes, missy.

A little later and darker, the fire enclosing **Lizzie** *and* **Robert**. *He reads, she makes measurements on a piece of transparent paper.*

Lizzie (*licking the pencil lead to encourage it*)   There's terrific burning in the wood, isn't there?

Robert (*half-attentive*)   Driftwood. (*Silence for a little, then, looking up.*) You know, they used to tie a lamp between the horns of a cow, and put it out to wander on Inch Strand, so that ships, trying to go up to Castlemaine Harbour, would take a course by it on a dark night, thinking it was a beacon, and run themselves on to the strand. There's many beds and tables in the houses around here that came out of such old ships. That was a savage thing to do, wasn't it? (*Back to his book.*)

Lizzie   The Gibsons did that?

Robert   No, no, the people, the people.

Lizzie   Oh, them. (*Marking the paper.*) I intend to make a good dress for Teresa. Why shouldn't she have a fine dress? She has a great interest in clothes. With her stature she could make her fortune as a child act. Singing, I mean. She could be a child till she was sixty, with the proper painting of her face. (*After a little.*) What are you reading?

Robert   Horace.

Lizzie   Oh, Horace. And what does he say, Horace?

Robert   What does he say? He recommends a life of narrow poverty. *Angustam pauperiam.*

Lizzie   Oh, that old thing.

Robert Which is just as well, Lizzie, because that's how we'll end up, the way things are going.

Lizzie Po – he recommends poverty? He doesn't know much about it, I think.

Robert Maybe so – his father was an auctioneer, right enough.

They laugh together.

Lizzie An auctioneer – good God! (*Goes on working for a little.*) I knew another man once that liked Horace. A big Scottish fellow, in the Presbyterian orphanage. He told us one time we were the future of Ireland. I can hear his lovely accent now. 'The roses of the Presbyterian Mission in the West.' A roomful of bony girls, gawping up at him. When I think of it. (*Holding up the paper.*) Would you look at poor Teresa, there's nothing to her.

Robert The future. So you are, Lizzie, I'm sure.

Lizzie Ho! Future. In those days it was my dream to go to America and marry a Redman and live in a wigwam in the wilderness. That didn't come to pass, did it?

Robert No, sadly.

Lucinda *appears rather suddenly upstage, looking a little lonesome and dishevelled.*

Lucinda Oh, here you are, of course. I got rather muddled. We're not in the drawing-room at this time of year. I will forget that.

Robert Mamma, dear, good evening.

Lucinda (*coming to the fire tentatively*) It's quite nice, isn't it, in here, with the fire lit. You always used to sit in here, the four of you, making a lot of noise talking and singing.

Lizzie Singing? (*To* **Robert**, *teasing.*) Hymns, was it?

Robert Mamma, come nearer to the fire here, it's blessed cold over by the door.

She approaches tentatively.

I like to listen to the sea as long as I can, and this is the best room for that, certainly.

Lucinda Do you remember playing croquet in here, with old Mrs Thomson's wool?

Robert No, I don't, Mamma.

Lucinda (*standing near the fire but awkwardly*) Your father wanted to remodel this room to look like a little side chapel in Christ Church Cathedral. I wouldn't have it. He said it looked like someone's tomb already and why not go the whole hog? Well, it was always very difficult to tell whether your father was being humorous or not.

Robert I hope he was being humorous on that occasion.

Lucinda The truth is, you know, my dear, I only miss your father at this – butt-end of the year. In the summer, well, somehow I blow along quite nicely. But just here, where the year turns so insidiously . . .

Robert He was always up the hillside this time of year, blasting the life out of little birds. I'm sure you never saw him.

Lucinda (*laughing*) Little birds. (*Laughing.*) The only other man who could ever make Lucinda Gibson chuckle was your great-uncle John Godfrey. He was an interesting man, Mrs Gibson. He helped to lay the telegraph cable across the Atlantic, it goes out there somewhere into the sea, by Ventry, is it, I forget? They wanted to knight him too, but he was much too immersed in his books. He used to sit in here in those old fled days, talking to your father and me. We thought him very romantic, with huge moustaches as was the fashion of the time. Yes, he put that heavy cable, cased in lead, he used to say, like a long thin grandee in his coffin, from here to New York, unwinding it off a big wheel on a neat little ship they had. And as soon as they had it laid down, why, the Irish deaths began to meet the American births running along the cable the other direction. You know? It was a triumph for him. How odd to think men like him can actually die. 'Isn't one bay enough, if it's your bay?' he used to say, when your father would be bemoaning the size of these lands, 'Isn't one bay enough,' as if, heaven knows, we owned the whole of Corcaguiney and the waters by it.

Robert   Well, he was certainly a favourite of yours, Mamma.

Lucinda   Oh, yes. Most definitely. If your father had had an ounce of his gusto, his learning, or his strength. Not that your father was a complete waste of time.

Lizzie   He gave you a nice enough son, Lady Gibson.

Lucinda   Jingo, he gave me four sons, the rogue. Well, I'll go up to my bed. I'm sorry to pester you with memories that are undoubtedly of no interest to you. You know how a human creature likes to talk of what it knows and knew. Goodnight, dear. Goodnight, Mrs Gibson.

Robert   Oh, I like to hear about the old fellows you had a bit of a *grá* for, Mamma.

Lucinda   I see. Goodnight. (*She goes.*)

Lizzie   Goodnight, Lady Gibson.

Robert *and* **Lizzie** *share a look.*

She detests me, would you say?

Robert   Not at all.

Lizzie   Why does the woman always call me Mrs Gibson? I never know who she's talking to. I look around for this Mrs Gibson.

Robert   She's very old-fashioned. That was the way of it in her generation. She used to call my father Mr Gibson.

Lizzie   She didn't!

Robert Oh, yes. Publicly, at any rate. If she felt really intimate, or was telling a story about him – because he went all over Corcaguiney as a magistrate, and was always courting disasters – if she was really being affectionate and warm towards him, she called him Magistrate.

Lizzie My God, Robert.

Robert Oh, yes. Just that touch formal, my Mamma. It was the fashion of manners in her young days. I don't think she notices how peculiar it sounds to our ears.

Lizzie Imagine me calling you Mr Gibson. May we go up to our doss now, Mr Gibson? Can we go up and have a good roll in the hay above, Mr Gibson?

Robert But of course, Mrs Gibson. My pleasure, I'm sure.

He leads her off as if to a dance.

Frosty daylight, **Bartholomew** *alone in the yard, raking the patch of gravel.* **Teresa** *comes on from the avenue. She's wearing a pair of old boots, which makes it hard for her to hurry. There's mud on her spindly legs.*

Bartholomew No coat, Teresa?

Teresa No, no, Barty. There's no fashion in my coat.

Bartholomew (*looking at her*) Fashion, is it? You were looked for earlier and not found. You were adjudged to be deep in your sculleries at your work, teeming potatoes and the like.

Teresa Oh, don't accuse me, Barty. I'll tell you where I was, if you can keep a priesteen's counsel.

Bartholomew That's not as secure as you may think, doty. Where were you so?

Teresa I was visiting my beau for five minutes.

Bartholomew In my old boots? Which one of your beaux, Teresa, girl?

Teresa The lovely pigman down at Kaiser Field. Oh. You won't say?

Bartholomew You'll need a tin bath and a strong nose if that's a marriage, doty. However did you keep those boots up on you?

Teresa I stuffed the blooming *Castlemaine Herald* into them!

She hurries up the steps and crosses the hall. **Lizzie** *and* **Robert**, *dressed for a walk, meet her halfway.*

Oh, Lord.

Robert Someone's looking for you, Teresa. Someone with a cross face.

Teresa Oh, Lord. (*Goes in.*)

They go down the steps to **Bartholomew**.

Bartholomew Good morning to you. I hope it's all going well for you. (**Lizzie** *smiles.* **Bartholomew** *gets quite jaunty.*) There's a touch of rain about, you may find. This hat hates rain.

Lizzie Does it?

Bartholomew You see that house-field lying fallow there?

Lizzie Yes.

Bartholomew There'd be a great frolic on that same field every August in the old days.

Lizzie Is that right?

Bartholomew Oh, yes. There's no market for hay now and if there was there'd be few enough men to work willingly for so little and so long.

Robert That's the truth, Bartholomew.

Bartholomew (*encouraged*) A field like that with no market for it would kill a small man beyond Ventry if it was his one and only field!

Lizzie Of course, it would, yes.

Bartholomew (*almost sweating*)   In former times, missy, the mistress of this house would come out from the house to the hay lying dry as dresses in that field, and take up the pitchfork like a very man and turn the first line to the sun for luck. For luck in the harvest and in the going-on of things.

Lizzie   Well, couldn't I come out next year, if you gave me the signal?

Bartholomew   Could you? Lucinda Gibson never did come out, and that was a pity.

Lizzie   If you give me the signal next year, I'm your girl.

Bartholomew   Every district has its custom by which a district endures. You must revere the custom of a place, or die away. You must turn the warm sheaves to the sun obediently, or die away.

A bit of a silence at this announcement.

Lizzie (*very seriously*)   Begod, Mr Grady. Thank you for sharing that with us.

Bartholomew (*subdued a little*)   My father used to say that to me. He got it out of Virgil, I believe.

Lizzie   Well, he was right, your father, he was right.

Bartholomew (*pleased*)   He was. Or was it Virgil was right?

Now, the falling September light on the strand. **Robert** *and* **Lizzie** *come down by the marram grass and the midden and walk a little downstage. The fresh sound of the waves running in broadly from Dingle Bay, the piping of birds.*

Robert   Did you notice that old midden there, Lizzie?

Lizzie   Where, sweet? That old heap of shells and such?

Robert   I met an Englishman on the strand years ago, who told me that midden was begun in the time of Christ. To think of people here all that while, living simply from the sea. Right down to the old picker of winkles who used to infest that little house by the strand.

Lizzie   A harsh cruel life, I'd say, out in the rain and the wind.

Robert   Of course, it would have been, yes. You're right, Lizzie.

Lizzie   People just like me in other days gone by, just like me, probably. Little hectic people that never heard of music-halls.

Robert   You think so? Maybe it was your crowd put the lamp on the cow so, and killed the poor mariners?

Lizzie   It does sound like something I'd do, you know. I didn't like to say last night, and spoil your story.

They wander away upstage and off. Just the emptiness and privacy of the strand for a little, with the subtle changes of light provided by the stirring sky. Gradually, the waltzing music of a little orchestra, distantly, the strand getting some hints of gold, and after a while, two splendid chandeliers lower and illumine the space, and now some couples appear, dressed richly and beautifully. The people themselves aren't as lovely as their clothes. **Lord Castlemaine**, *a tall powerful-looking man, dances with his wife,* **Lady Castlemaine**, *who is plump but energetic. Great glitter and appearance of happiness. A little* **Factotum**, *dressed blackly, is taking cards. Now* **Lizzie** *and* **Robert**, *looking splendid,* **Lizzie** *in her very best red dress, approach the* **Factotum**, *who takes their card balefully.*

Factotum   Mr and Mrs Robert Godfrey Gibson!

The dance continues, **Lady Castlemaine** *watching* **Lizzie** *as she looks on eagerly.* **Lizzie** *smiles up at* **Robert**. *Even* **Robert** *seems stirred. The dance ends,* **Lady Castlemaine** *whispers something to her husband and goes upstage to speak to one of the other women.* **Lord Castlemaine** *crosses to* **Robert**.

Lord Castlemaine   Gibson, how nice to see you. We heard you were about again. How splendid you could come tonight. (*Shakes his hand.*)

Robert   You haven't met my wife, Lizzie.

Lord Castlemaine   No, I haven't. And it's a great pleasure. We heard that Robert had found himself a great – a great actress.

Robert   Lord Castlemaine – Lizzie Gibson.

Lizzie   How do you do, Lord Castlemaine? I was never a great actress, I'm sad to say.

Lord Castlemaine (*taking her hand*)   You must never think we are so provincial here as not to honour the stage. We hear a great deal about the stage that is unsavoury, and we know it is bunkum. After all, my dear, Shakespeare himself was an actor.

Lizzie   I'm proud enough to have known the stage life, I must admit.

Lord Castlemaine   Excellent, excellent. I want you two to enjoy yourselves. My wife, Lady Castlemaine, took a good look at you, Mrs Gibson, while she danced, and whispered in my ear that you would do very well. I want you to know that. She can tell whether a person will wash or not from two hundred yards, if needs be.

Lizzie   That's a talent, Lord Castlemaine.

Lord Castlemaine   There now, Gibson. I haven't offended, I hope?

Robert   No, no.

Lord Castlemaine *heads back to his wife.*

(*To* **Lizzie**.) The bloody fool.

Lord Castlemaine *turns again, a notion striking him.*

Lord Castlemaine   I would so like to talk to you, Gibson – about Africa.

Robert   Oh, yes. Not a lot to say, really.

Lord Castlemaine   Oh, I think there is a little to say. In a while, in a while.

He heads over to his wife again. The music begins.

(*Over his shoulder.*) And I'll have a dance with you, Mrs Gibson, if you don't mind your feet crushed!

Lizzie (*to* **Robert**) Well?

Robert   You'd like to . . .

Lizzie   I'll kill myself if you don't. A dance to me is like raw meat to a lion.

Robert   I'd never disappoint a hungry lion, Lizzie.

They join in the dance. It's true that **Lizzie** *never looked happier than when she dances now, unless it was doing the cancan with* **Jelly Jane**. **Robert** *and she are swept into a feeling of great union by the music, as good as a marriage. Now the* **Factotum** *pulls onstage a long table piled with food, covered in an immaculate white tablecloth, trimmed with the colours of the Castlemaines. The inhabitants of the countryside seem to have found their way on to the plates, along with much beef and puddings and wines. The people gather in to eat, helped to food by the* **Factotum**.

Lizzie (*whispering to* **Robert**)   If my father had ever seen a spread-out like that, he'd of sang like a linnet all night in hopes of a go at it.

Robert (*laughing*)   You can eat for him so. In his memory.

Lizzie   I will, Robert, I will. That's a fine compliment to him. Thank you. (*She goes with her plate to the* **Factotum**.)

Factotum   Is it most things you're after?

Lizzie   Oh, yes. Most things will do nicely. Everything will do better.

Factotum   Sure I'll give you everything so. Quail?

Lizzie   Oh, yes.

Factotum   You know the noise that fella makes?

Lizzie   No. (**Factotum** *does it.*) Remarkable.

Factotum   Partridge?

Lizzie   Oh, yes, lovely.

Factotum (*serving it*)   You know . . . (**Lizzie** *shakes her head nay. The* **Factotum** *does the sound of the partridge.*) Pheasant?

Lizzie   Yes. (*He does the pheasant.*) You know, you remind me of a man I knew once in the music-hall. You're the very spit of him. You don't know the birds of Ohio, by any chance, do you?

Factotum   No, ma'am, only the birds of Corcaguiney.

Lady Castlemaine *approaches* **Lizzie**.

Lady Castlemaine   Hello, my dear. My husband tells me you are perfectly delightful, and so I see you are. Isn't Peadar a wonder with his bird calls?

Lizzie   He is – just wonderful.

Lady Castlemaine   I told him when you arrived at Red House it wasn't the first time there was wild blood into Corcaguiney. People forget it now, because it suits them to forget, but my grandmother was a very beautiful woman who came from the very darkest thickets of Portugal. And, my dear, would you believe it, was one of those fanatical Catholics who were brought up never to talk to a Protestant if they could help it. She was reared by the Princess of Brazil in Lisbon, and really was the most wonderful, bigoted woman I ever knew. Even at ninety-three.

Lizzie *doesn't know how to take this.*

Am I being a fool? Am I bungling everything? I do bungle things so.

Lizzie   I know you mean it kindly, it's just – I'm not bigoted and I'm not Portuguese.

Lady Castlemaine   I know, I know. Come with me, Mrs Gibson, and I'll show you her picture in the hall. Then we can get back to dancing, when our supper has settled.

Lizzie (*going off with her*)   It'll take a good while enough for these poor birds to settle.

Lady Castlemaine (*disappearing*)   The main thing is, my dear, for people to remain in their houses, to hold to Corcaguiney, make their stand here, if they can . . .

Robert *and* **Lord Castlemaine** *together now.*

Lord Castlemaine   I just wanted to say, Gibson, I was very put out to hear about your brothers. Very much so. I was very fond of them all. As you know my own father fought in the Crimea. I feel a great kinship with your mother and you in your sorrow.

Robert   It's not as simple as that, of course.

Lord Castlemaine   No, indeed not, and this is no place to discuss war. But it's been on my mind to write to you. I wrote to your mother at the time.

Robert   I'm sure that was very thoughtful of you.

Lord Castlemaine   Let me say, and God knows you've the right to shut me up if you wish, but though they died, they died well, they died for these three kingdoms and in service of their great Queen. And you survive now, noble and good, having done your utmost and given your all for the same immortal lady.

Robert (*quietly*)   You shouldn't assume, Lord Castlemaine.

Lord Castlemaine   Excuse me?

Robert   I simply say, you shouldn't presume.

Lord Castlemaine   How so, Gibson?

Robert   It's true Frank and Harry died as nobly as people can die, when your general is a fool, and your cause is unjust.

Lord Castlemaine   Unjust!

Robert   I resigned my commission two years ago after they were so wastefully killed. Wastefully.

Lord Castlemaine   What?

Robert   They never even saw the Boer guns that killed them. They were found in the morning with their companions all dusty and dead in the brushwood, half-eaten by the wild dogs of Africa.

Lord Castlemaine   War's not pretty, Gibson. You know that. And Charles? Did Charles also resign his commission? He died, didn't he, wearing his uniform?

Robert   Charlie died of drink in Cape Town. That's how he took the news. He died in my arms screaming blue murder and seeing demons. Not a pretty death, really. But, in his uniform.

Lord Castlemaine (*after a moment*)   I did assume, didn't I? So dreadfully assume. (*Touches* **Robert**'*s arm.*)

Robert   I resigned my commission and shortly afterwards accepted a captaincy in the Boer army. I crossed to Kruger, as it were. His Irish Brigade, to be exact.

Lord Castlemaine (*after a moment, taking back his hand*)   That rabble?

Lizzie *and* **Lady Castlemaine** *join them.*

Lady Castlemaine   I showed her that wild grandmother of mine, Henry. She said she looked a bit peaky, didn't you, my dear? (*Catching the atmosphere.*)

Lord Castlemaine   These ruffians going about with guns, shooting landlords, and burning haycocks, they're all pro-Boer.

Robert   I think I can make a distinction between Africa and Ireland.

Lord Castlemaine   I hope you can. You must go now from my house. After we made an effort for this, this woman you've married.

Lady Castlemaine   What do you mean, dear? What's the matter?

Lord Castlemaine   We've been duped. Gibson has changed camps, you might say, haven't you, Gibson? He fought for the Boers!

Lady Castlemaine   I should think that's his business.

Lord Castlemaine   Well, really, my dear Lady
Castlemaine, you are unshockable. But I am not. A man who
is pro-Boer can eat his supper somewhere else. And take his
dancing woman with him.

Lady Castlemaine   I don't think you want to say that,
dear.

Robert   It's all right, Lady Castlemaine.

Lizzie   It isn't all right so much as you think, Robert.

Robert   It's all right, in the sense that we are going now.

Lizzie   There's many in England itself that were against
that war without being against the soldiers.

Lord Castlemaine   Against the war without being against
the soldiers? What sort of way is that to lead your life?
They're all mad in England, I've always said so!

Robert   Come along with me, Lizzie Finn, and don't be
fighting with him. He's not up to your mettle.

They head off undaunted. **Lizzie** *turns briefly to* **Lord
Castlemaine**.

Lizzie   I won't have that dance with you now – if you don't
mind.

Deep November, **Robert** *tucked in by the fire reading.* **Teresa**
*stands on a chair in the middle of the hall, wearing the new dress,
while* **Lizzie** *pins gold and silk trim on to it intently.*

Robert (*to himself, reading*)   What ought I say of autumn's
storms and stars?

Teresa (*seeing a fallen heap of books beside* **Lizzie***'s chair, and one
open on the seat itself*)   You like to deck the books, missy,
that's for certain.

Lizzie   I never had much time for them in olden days. I've taken a run at them now and I'll be hard to stop. I've read even manuals of grainstores and books about the care of forests in India.

Teresa And what's that little fellow there you're looking at?

Lizzie It's not one of the house, but one that Robert fetched home for me. It's called *The Only True History of Frank James, by Himself.* It's a mighty book about an outlaw in America, penned mightily by the man himself. He robbed great gobs of gold off trains and rode hard through the days with his brother Jesse. He's a man to like. Robert, who is a scholar, says Frank James never did write any book and it only says he did to make you believe it's the plain truth. I believe Robert, and I believe the book. It's wild and exciting, with guns and good times and running from the laws.

Teresa Now, that would be a tale for Teresa.

Lizzie You could steal it to your room after me.

Teresa I would but, no shame to me, I've no letters. Lady wrote my name into my shifts and knickers when I came first. I hadn't the wit to tell her it was no advantage to me. I was young then, missy. I half-know my own letters. I'm staring at them often enough when the linen comes back from the laundry girls. Barty swore one time he'd teach me, but his pots and blooms have first call on Barty. Missy?

Lizzie Yes, dear?

Teresa Was it wild good at the Castlemaines' ball, tell us.

Lizzie It was wild good, wasn't it, Robert?

Robert Wild good.

Teresa I heard so. My mother's always at me, at me, to get employment at Lady Castlemaine's. She does the dairy for them there. The maiding, you know.

Lizzie Well, girl – maybe you will.

A longish pause. **Teresa** *not moving. Suddenly she's crying.*

Teresa You don't think the pigman will have me so!

Lizzie Oh, I do, I do!

Teresa   What would be the point of the dress otherwise? I might as well wear flour-sacks.

Robert   Shush now, Teresa, in the house.

Lizzie   Shush now.

Teresa   Oh, it's a lovely dress, and what you put on there. Gold ribbon! I never even laid eyes on gold ribbon before. And the square of satin there on my poor flat bosom. Who'd a credited Teresa with such an immensity of a dress? Of course, it won't impress Barty.

Lizzie   It does suit you, girl. I'm glad you like it. You can sew in the bits yourself.

Teresa   Amn't I delightful in this? (*Dancing a bit on the chair.*) Someday I'll get shoes for this in Tralee, and then God help the pigman. (*An inspiration.*) I know the perfect complement for this missy, I do! (*She leaps from the chair, heads off into the house.*)

Lizzie   Mind the pins, girl, mind the pins! (*To* **Robert**, *laughing.*) She's a lovely wild girl.

Robert   She's like two buckets banging together!

Lucinda *comes in slowly. She carries her prayerbook and gloves and was obviously out at chapel. She seems dazed.*

Are you all right, Mamma?

Lucinda (*stuck at the door*)   Curious, curious. I only wished to attend evensong. I drove myself in the trap, quite independently, quite happily. Frosty and pleasant the countryside looked. I thought of myself sitting among the other worshippers, clean and starched and pleasant, our girls singing in the gallery. The clockwork, the rightness of it all. The truth of it. All simplified before God by the singing. The balm that has been given to me.

Robert   What happened, Mamma?

Lucinda   The face of the rector surprised me. He was standing inside the doors, looking at me in horror. I thought it was a trick of the light, of the November light. Like a stone face in the shadows. Suddenly I thought some tragedy had befallen him, some terrible event, his wife was dead, his daughters had been taken . . . I hurried to him. I hurried to my doom!

Robert   Mamma, Mamma.

Lucinda   He's such a pale-faced creature, with that singsonging voice. He said things to me that seemed terrible and stark from his lips. Things that seemed shocking to me suddenly, that seemed to freeze my heart, as if bags of summer ice were stacked about it. Things I knew, or I thought I knew, that seemed suddenly more terrible to me than death, more shocking than death. Because he was describing to me the death of truth and rightness in my own house.

Robert   No, Mamma.

Lucinda   Described those things to me, and seemed to bar me from entering, from joining the worshippers all dark within, my refuge, Robert. I drove back along the sea road like a ghost. Coldness is an illness like to cholera, it kills and infects. I am so cold.

Teresa *bursts back into the room triumphantly, hardly seeing* **Lucinda**. *She rushes centrestage, alive with her inspiration.*

Teresa   See, missy, see, the perfect complement!

She hoists her new dress violently, to show **Lizzie** *the starry knickers.*

Later, **Robert** *and* **Lizzie** *alone by the fire.*

Robert   It was a wicked thing to do, wicked. To keep her from the chapel.

Lizzie   But she knew about me, and she knew about Africa, didn't she?

Robert   Knowing it, and being told about it, may be different things. It's your money paid down the debts of this house, and the real scandal is the level of debts allowed to us after the farms were sold. I hate to put capital to debts rather than income, but there it is. She's secure for the first time in many a long year, and if I can correctly revolutionise the farms remaining and start us back to health, she'll be securer still. Maybe it's time she stopped imagining herself the Queen of Corcaguiney. Though I wouldn't chose such a method to sear off her wings.

Lizzie   Her face was ashen. I never saw the like before.

Robert   She's terrified. If you don't have visits and visiting in a district like this, you may go mad, I suppose.

Lizzie   It was all her world to be Queen of Corcaguiney, I see that.

Robert   Why are they so ruled by imaginary distinctions? In this wild place? Well, I suppose it's because I crossed to the Boers.

Lizzie   God knows, doty, a man that has lost three brothers can do what he likes.

Robert   The fact of it is, crossing to Kruger healed nothing. If your heart is almost broken, a change of uniform is a poor bandage. I don't know what bearing it has on my mother. Why did they go for her?

Lizzie   So they all may feel at home. I'll go up to her.

Robert   Do, Lizzie, do. That's kind.

Upstage, **Lucinda** *standing in front of* **Lizzie.** **Lucinda** *holds a dress across her arms.*

Lizzie   I've brought great grief to you. I'm sorry for it.

Lucinda   There's nothing to be done, and you are just what you are, and clear about it, and I have been foolish after my own fashion.

Lizzie   Not foolish at all.

Lucinda   Look, I was to give this to you at Christmastide, but I prefer to give it now, if I may.

Lizzie (*taking the dress*)   Thank you. It is so sombre and elegant. Thank you for a beautiful dress.

Lucinda   Why wouldn't I buy my own daughter a dress, Mrs Gibson?

Lizzie   It seems to me Spanish somehow. Like in the picture-book about the Moors in the library – the deep current of blue in the dark cloth.

Lucinda   Of course, it may be.

Lizzie   Well, well, thank you again.

Lucinda (*turning away*)   Do not think you are not loved in this house.

The light of the fire washing in on **Robert**, *his face lit. Faintly, fractured, the voice of a man singing from an operetta, to which* **Robert** *pays no heed.*

The next day, a cold blank November day. **Bartholomew** *works at inserting kindling under his bonfire, it's arduous for him to stoop, but he's absorbed in the work. He's looking forward to the flames.*

Bartholomew   The fire will wake flies nearby in the stones, but it will be a false awakening.

Lucinda *comes down the steps. She doesn't look at* **Bartholomew,** *which surprises him.*

Good morning, lady.

Lucinda (*vaguely*)   Yes, Bartholomew.

She goes on right and exits downstage. **Bartholomew** *returns to his task. He strikes a Lucifer and tries the kindling, watches the nest of flames grow. But something bothers him. He keeps looking after* **Lucinda.** *He goes a little right and looks down over the strand.*

Bartholomew   There she goes. (*Watches another while, now and then glancing back at the growing bonfire. Suddenly, in some alarm.*) Lady! Lady! She can't hear me! Mr Robert! (*No response.*) Lady! Don't! She's walked straight in! Oh, lady! (*He follows after, off.*)

The bonfire brightly.

Some days later. **Robert** *looking famished in the hall, reading a telegram.* **Lizzie** *comes in, then* **Teresa.**

Robert (*reading*)   Robert Godfrey Gibson, Esq., Red House. (*To* **Lizzie** *and* **Teresa,** *who hold each other's hands.*) It's from the captain of the light-house at Dunquin. (*Reading.*) Sea-coves beyond Dingle. Black dress. (*To* **Lizzie** *and* **Teresa.**) Yes, she's found. (*Reading.*) Difficult news . . . Tides – yes, I agree with him. Sea calm. Freak wave . . . (*To himself.*) I don't know, I don't know. (*To* **Lizzie** *and* **Teresa.**) No sign of Bartholomew Grady. (*Reading.*) Seen by old woman, strand, swimming out . . . (*To himself.*) Indeed, very courageous, very. (*To* **Lizzie** *and* **Teresa.**) The carters in Dingle will bring her up to the house. (*Lowers the telegram.*) Very well. We'll be expecting them. Some hours yet. I must thank the captain for his kindness. (*To* **Lizzie** *and* **Teresa.**) Please don't worry. Nothing to be done, my dears.

Teresa *holds on to* **Lizzie.**

Teresa (*very quietly*)   It was me, wasn't it, missy? With the knickers?

Lizzie (*equally quietly*)   Never and no, sweet, never and no.

Later, **Lizzie** *on her knees trying to light the hall fire, there's a knack to it that eludes her.* **Robert** *comes up the steps with a few letters. He sees her at the fire, doesn't speak for a moment.*

Robert   Well. Is Teresa not about?

Lizzie   She's quite destitute. Everything here reminds her of one or other of them. I sent her down to Kaiser Field where she has a friend. (*Seeing the letters.*) What are they?

Robert   Condolences. There's a quite charming one from Johnson the fuel merchant in Castlemaine. In his very best schoolroom writing. (*Shows a letter.*) This one with the crest, is from Lord Castlemaine.

Lizzie   What does he want?

Robert   Oh, it's as formal as a hedge. I suppose he thinks he was Mamma's great friend.

Lizzie   I bet he does. (*Rising.*) I don't understand this fire. I don't.

Robert   Nobody does except Teresa.

The next day, a little reception in the hall after **Lucinda***'s funeral. It's subdued enough.* **Lord** *and* **Lady Castlemaine** *with the* **Rector, Lizzie** *in the dress* **Lucinda** *gave her,* **Robert** *in black clothes.* **Teresa** *looking terrified and useless by the door.* **Robert** *takes the tray from her, and pours a dark sherry into the little glasses the guests are clutching, like straws.*

Lizzie (*the* **Rector** *bears a great resemblance to the* **Factotum**)
You don't know the birds of Ohio, do you?

The **Rector** *looks at her.*

Rector (*quickly*)   I don't think I do, Mrs Gibson.

Lizzie (*to herself*)   Some day, somewhere, someone's going to call me Lizzie again.

Lord Castlemaine   Our man tells us there's a storm brewing down there in the bay. We don't want to be blown about the sea-road. We won't stay long. A lovely sherry, I must say.

Lizzie   Portuguese.

Lady Castlemaine   Really?

Lord Castlemaine   I must say, we expected a bit of a gathering. It's not like the old days, is it? You'd find a hundred mourners and more at a funeral, a hundred and more.

Robert   Oh, we might have had a few others, I suppose. My agent couldn't come down from Tralee, as it happens. But we thought the three of you would like to pay your respects properly, in the house itself.

Lord Castlemaine   Oh, indeed. I relish the opportunity. Very well put, Gibson. Indeed. Wasn't it, Lady Castlemaine?

Lady Castlemaine   It was, my dear.

Robert   She had few enough close friends in these later years. She was content to stay at home since Papa died. But loved to visit when she was able. When she was asked.

Lord Castlemaine   Of course.

Robert   I am just glad you let her lie inside the walls of the yard, rector. We must be grateful to the captain of the Dunquin Light and his theory of waves.

Rector   A freak wave is not as uncommon as people believe, I think.

Lord Castlemaine   Not at all as uncommom. They're an everyday occurrence, in fact. They really shouldn't be called freak at all.

Robert   Just waves, in fact.

Lord Castlemaine   Indeed. Waves. Waves.

At the door **Teresa** *hangs her head quietly and beings to cry. The* **Rector** *and the* **Castlemaines** *look at her.* **Lizzie** *goes and puts an arm about her.*

Lizzie (*softly*)   There, doty, don't cry. You go to your pigman and don't mind this here. (**Teresa** *looks up at her.*) Go on.

Teresa *escapes.* **Lizzie** *walks back towards the guests.*

Lady Castlemaine (*to* **Lizzie**)   They're so devoted, the people.

Lizzie *gives her an odd smile and goes on across the hall and down the step.*

She has a little bit of blue in her dress. I didn't like to say. It bothered me.

Robert *looks at her long and hard.*

A little later, **Lizzie** *at the left of the strand.*

Lizzie   Just sometimes, wouldn't you like to shoot people?

Robert *comes up behind her and puts a coat about her shoulders. She turns, remembers the coat in the music hall, laughs.*

That's the second time, my love.

Robert   What did you say, Lizzie?

Lizzie   Nothing – only blathering.

Robert   I'm sorry about that trio of lunatics. I shouldn't have asked them.

Lizzie   Oh, it doesn't matter, Robert. I wanted to get down to the strand before nightfall anyway. Did I ever show you this yoke?

She takes the stone angel from a pocket, and kneels to bury it in the sand.

Robert   What is it?

Lizzie   It's an old angel that Jelly Jane gave me, that her father dug up somewhere. It was to give to our child, should he show his nose, or she. (**Robert** *laughs.*) I hope she won't mind me putting it in here.

Robert   Why are you putting it there, Lizzie?

Lizzie   For your mother. It's a Yorkshire angel, and she was from Yorkshire, wasn't she?

Robert   Yes, she was.

Lizzie *rises, knocking the sand off her hands.*

Lizzie   There. It's not a very big monument, I suppose, not like you see on some of those tomb-houses in the yard at Castlemaine. Big, black-looking angels with wings the size of yachts.

Robert   It's a splendid monument. Mamma never had a *grá* for tombs. That's why we had her put under the yews, with a decent view down the bay to Inch.

Lizzie   For heaven's sake, sure you'd want that. At the very least. She was most of her life gawping down at it from the house there.

Robert   Exactly. Here. (*Fetching out something of his own from a little container, a vade-mecum.*) Put that in for Bartholomew.

Lizzie   What is it so?

Robert Did you never wonder what happened to it? I even chose a little box for it, a vade-mecum, Lizzie, to protect me from my own foolishness. The hatpin. The sacred hatpin.

Lizzie All right. (*Putting it in the sand. After a little.*) Well, Mr Gibson, what are we going to do for friends here?

Robert. I do not know.

Lizzie A girl likes to have great pals, you know. I suppose we could grow old and curmudgeonly and see no one and fill the house with scalded-looking brats and love them hugely, a little tribe of rasher-faced Gibsons.

Robert We mightn't have a choice. I don't see us dancing with the Castlemaines too often.

Lizzie God forbid! I would rather kill myself than dance with them, Robert Gibson!

Robert Ah. Lizzie, Lizzie, I've lead you astray to this useless place.

Lizzie No, heart. All the places of the world, where things are expected of a person, are the same. I'll call it home where Robert is, if you'll do the same. What's our history, Robert, but something like that poor Frank James had, a true history of lies, and written by nobody, as you told me yourself? There'll be nobody in the wide world to remember us, child, and all that will remain of us is an echo, a strain of dancing music, and the memory of a man that loved his brothers and his people, who was given a heart as restless as a frightened dog by wars and accidents. So what odds where we are?

Robert Perhaps we could make a better life for ourselves somewhere else?

Lizzie I've sometimes wondered why you needed to come back here at all. Apart from Lucinda.

Robert Love of the place. And it was mine, of course.

Lizzie That's good enough reason. I'm willing to stay on and be rude to as many toffs as I need to be. I am.

Robert   I know. But you wouldn't really like it. I feel different about things now, with you. I'm not so keen to be at home. I'd rather be a foreigner some place. Like Cork, for instance.

Lizzie   Cork? (*Laughs.*) Well, they have a new music-hall there in Cork, I was reading.

Robert   I was reading too.

Lizzie   It's the scandal of the *Castlemaine Herald*. We could try our luck there. And I'd be a fierce respectable act, married to you. They'll think I'm proper royalty. I could ask for some shocking rates, I could. And if I am a bit long in the tooth for showing my legs, couldn't I take up with the singing?

Robert   Oh, I should stick with the dancing . . . (*Lizzie gives him a puck.*) I don't mind the sound of that. I can't be a farmer if there's no farms. I don't fancy falling into the sea with poor Red House. Better go off now while the going's good.

Lizzie   Mr Gibson, you're a man to gladden my heart.

Robert   We'll just spend the one last night up in the linen bed, and get that train in the evening tomorrow. The agent in Tralee can try and sell the place for us. We'll just walk out the blessed door and turn the old key in the lock. Why not?

The pull of the wind about them, drawing them closer.

Lizzie   Is it very far to Cork from here, Mr Gibson?

They're walking off slowly left.

Robert   I believe it's a terrible distance, Mrs Gibson.

Lizzie   And are they very wild there? I've heard it said.

Robert   Oh, they are, I'm sure.

Lizzie   It will suit us so.

Echo of a song from an operetta. The wind about them. She includes him in her coat. They go off. Curtain.

The Steward of Christendom

For Donal

Characters

Thomas Dunne, *early to mid seventies at the time of the play, 1932*
Smith, *fiftyish*
Mrs O'Dea, *likewise or older*
Recruit, *eighteen*
Willie Dunne, *Thomas's son, born late 1890s, died in the First World War, thirteen or so as he appears in the play to Thomas, his voice not yet broken*
Annie Dunne, *Thomas's middle daughter, bowed back, about twenty in 1922, thirtyish 1932*
Maud Dunne, *Thomas's eldest daughter, early twenties in 1922*
Dolly Dunne, *Thomas's youngest daughter, about seventeen in 1922*
Matt Kirwin, *Maud's suitor and husband, mid to late twenties in 1922, mid to late thirties in 1932*

The play is set in the county home in Baltinglass, County Wicklow, in about 1932.

The Steward of Christendom was first performed in the Royal Court Theatre Upstairs, London, on 30 March 1995, with the following cast:

Thomas	Donal McCann
Smith	Kieran Ahern
Mrs O'Dea	Maggie McCarthy
Recruit	Rory Murray
Willie	Jonathan Newman
Annie	Tina Kellegher
Maud	Cara Kelly
Dolly	Aislín McGuckin
Matt	Rory Murray

Director Max Stafford-Clark
Designer Julian McGowan
Lighting Designer Johanna Town
Music Shaun Davey
Sound Designer Paul Arditti
Stage Management Rob Young, Sally McKenna, Caroline Boocock
Costume Supervisor Jennifer Cook
Production Electrician Matthew O'Connor

Act One

Circa 1932. **Thomas**'s *bare room in the county home in Baltinglass. A toiling music-hall music distantly. A poor table, an iron bed with a thin mattress and yellowing sheets. A grey blanket, a three-legged stool. A poor patch of morning light across* **Thomas**, *a solitary man of seventy-five, in the bed. His accent is south-west Wicklow, with his words clear.*

Thomas   Da Da, Ma Ma, Ba Ba, Ba Ba. Clover, clover in my mouth, clover honey-smelling, clover smelling of Ma Ma's neck, and Ma Ma's soft breast when she opens her floating blouse, and Da Da's bright boots in the grasses, amid the wild clover, and the clover again, and me the Ba Ba set in the waving grasses, and the smell of honey, and the farmhands going away like an army of redcoats but without the coats, up away up the headland with their scythes, and every bit of the sun likes to run along the scythes and laugh along the blades, now there are a score of shining scythes, dipping and signalling from the backs of the men.

A sharp banging on the door.

Smith   Wakey, wakey!

Thomas   Who is there?

Smith   Black Jim. Black Jim in the morning.

Thomas   Oh, don't come in, Black Jim, with your blackthorn stick raised high.

Smith   It's Black Jim.

Thomas   But don't you come in. There's no need. Is it Da Da?

Smith   It's Black Jim, and he must come in.

Thomas   There's no need. Thomas sleepy sleepy, beddy bye. Is it Da Da? (*No answer. More distantly on other doors there's a banging and the same 'Wakey, wakey' receding.*) Da Da comes in,

Da Da comes in, Tom no sleepy, Tom no sleepy. Tom you sleep, says Da Da, or you get big stick. And when little Tom no sleepy sleep, big stick comes in and hitting Tom Tommy, but now the polished boots are gone, and the dark has closed over the fields, and the smell of the clover is damped down now by summer cold, and the dress of Ma Ma hangs on the chair, and her face is pressed into the goosey pillow, and all is silence in the wooden world of the house, except the tread of the Da Da, a-worrying, a-worrying, except the fall of the big stick, cut from the blackthorn tree in the hushed deeps of winter. Da Da is golden, golden, golden, nothing that Da Da do takes away the sheen and the swoon of gold.

He bestirs himself, wipes his big hands on his face vigorously, gets out of bed with good strength. He is big-framed but diminished by age, in a not-too-clean set of long johns.

You bloody mad old man. Gabbling and affrighting yourself in the dark. Baltinglass, Baltinglass, that's where you are. For your own good, safe from harm. Like the milking cow taken down from the sloping field when the frost begins to sit on her tail. When her shit is frosty. Snug in the byre. (*He sits on the stool and leans in to the table as if pressing his face against the cow.*) Come to it, Daisy now, give your milk. Go on. (*Slaps a leg.*) Ah, Daisy, Daisy, sweet, give it up, for Thomas. Oh. (*As if getting a jet into the bucket.*) Oh, oh. (*Happily.*) Aye. (*Catching himself, stopping.*) The county home in Baltinglass, that's where you're situated. Seventy-five summers on your head and mad as a stone mason. Safe, safe, safety, safe, safe, safety, mad as a barking stone mason. Because you were not civil to your daughter, no, you were not. You were ranting, you were raving, and so they put you where you were safe. Like a dog that won't work without using his teeth, like a dog under sentence. But please do not you talk to Black Jim, Thomas, please do not, there's the manny. Because he is not there. (*Singing.*) There was an old woman that lived in the wood, willa, willa, wallya.

His own silence.

Da Da?

Mrs O'Dea, *the seamstress, a small plump woman in an ill-made dress and a white apron with big pockets full of tape and needles and oddments of black cloth, opens the door with her key and comes in.*

Mrs O'Dea (*a local accent*) Will you let me measure you today, Mr Dunne?

Thomas What for indeed?

Mrs O'Dea You can't wear those drawers forever.

Thomas I won't need to, Mrs O'Dea, I won't live forever.

Mrs O'Dea And what will you do when summer's gone? How can you bear to wear rags?

Thomas I rarely go out, you see.

Mrs O'Dea Look at the state of yourself. You're like something in a music-hall. Mrs Forbes, the Boneless Wonder, or some such.

Thomas This is a madhouse, it suits me to look like a madman while I'm here.

Mrs O'Dea If you allow me measure you, I'll make up a fine suit for you, as good as my own attire.

Thomas With that black cloth you use for all the poor men?

Mrs O'Dea Yes and indeed, it must be black, by regulation of the board.

Thomas If you had a bit of gold or suchlike for the thread, something to perk the suit up, why then, Mrs O'Dea, I would let you measure me.

Mrs O'Dea Gold thread? I have none of that, Mr Dunne.

Thomas That's my bargain. Take it or leave it.

Mrs O'Dea Would a yellow do?

Thomas Yes, yes.

Mrs O'Dea You're not afraid of looking like a big goose?

Thomas   I go out but rarely. If I look like a goose, few will see me. (*As an inspiration.*) I won't venture out at Christmas!

Mrs O'Dea (*taking out her measuring tape*)   Have you fleas?

Thomas   No, madam.

Mrs O'Dea (*calling out the door*)   Mr Smith! (*To* **Thomas**.) You won't mind Mr Smith washing you, just a little.

Thomas (*anxiously*)   Don't let Black Jim in here. Don't let him, for I've no sugar lumps. It's only sugar lumps appeases him.

Mrs O'Dea   He must wash you, Mr Dunne. It's just Mr Smith. You smell like a piece of pork left out of the dripping press, man dear.

Smith, *about fifty, balding, with the cheerfulness about him of the powerful orderly, comes in with a basin.*

Smith   Raise 'em.

Thomas (*backing away*)   The blackthorn stick hurts Tommy Tom. Sugar lumps, sugar lumps!

Mrs O'Dea   Take off your old long johns, and be easy in yourself. It's only a sponging.

Thomas (*trying to hold his clothes fast*)   Tum tum tum, bum bum bum.

Smith *roughly unbuttons the long johns and pulls them off,* **Thomas** *miserably covering himself.*

Smith   I'd a mind once to join my brother on the Hudson river. He has a whale flensing business there, flourishing. Would that I had joined Jack, I say, when I have to wash down an old bugger like you. I would rather flense whales, and that's a stinking task, I'm told.

Thomas (*smiling red-faced at* **Mrs O'Dea**)   Da Da.

Mrs O'Dea (**Smith** *beginning to sponge*)   Good man yourself, Mr Dunne.

Thomas (*weeping*)   Da Da, Ma Ma, Ba Ba.

Mrs O'Dea   My, my, that's a fine chest you have on you, Mr Dunne. What was your work formerly? I know you've told me often enough.

Thomas (*proudly enough*)   I was a policeman.

Mrs O'Dea   You had the chest for it.

Thomas   I had, madam.

Smith (*sponging*)   Dublin Metropolitan Police, weren't you, boyo? In your braid. The DMP, that are no more. Oh, la-di-da. Look at you.

Thomas (*smiling oddly*)   La-di-da.

Smith (*sponging*)   Castle Catholic bugger that you were. But you're just an old bastard in here with no one to sponge you but Smith.

Thomas   Black Jim no like Tommy Tom. No like Tommy Tom.

Smith   Chief superintendent, this big gobshite was, Mrs O'Dea, that killed four good men and true in O'Connell Street in the days of the lock-out. Larkin. Hah? His men it was struck down the strikers. (*A gentle hit with the drying cloth.*) Baton-charging. A big loyal Catholic gobshite killing poor hungry Irishmen. If you weren't an old madman we'd flay you.

Mrs O'Dea   That's fine, Mr Smith, leave him be. Can't you see you terrorise him? That's him scrubbed.

Smith (*going off with the basin*)   Excusing my language.

Mrs O'Dea   Can you put on your own clothes, Mr Dunne?

Thomas   I can, madam.

Mrs O'Dea   Is it true you gave your previous suit to a man in the walking meadow?

Thomas   It is. (*Dressing.*)

Mrs O'Dea   Why would you do a thing like that, and go in those rags yourself? Was the man you gave it to cold?

Thomas   No. He was hungry.

Mrs O'Dea   There's no eating in a suit, man dear.

Thomas   I was out a-walking in the lunatics' meadow, and Patrick O'Brien asked me for the suit. He was in former times the finest thrower of the bullet in Kiltegan. Do you know what a bullet is? It is a ball of granite whittled down in an evening by a boy. I could tell you tales of Patrick O'Brien and the bullet, on the roads there round about. All the men of the village milling there, raging to win fame at the bulleting if God shone the light of luck on them, the thrower slowly slowly raising the bullet, slowly dipping it, then away, with a great fling of the arm, down the road with it, and well beyond the next corner if he could. And if the bullet touched the grassy marge, a terrible groan would issue from the man and his supporters. And the young boys red in the face from ambition and desire. Patrick O'Brien, a tall yellow streak of a man now, that thinks he is a dog. A dog, Mrs O'Dea. When he asked for the suit, I couldn't refuse him, for memory of his great skill. They were evenings any human person would remember.

Mrs O'Dea (*measuring him now with the tape, putting up his arms and so on as necessary*)   What did he want with your suit?

Thomas   To eat, he said. To bury it and eat it, piecemeal, as the spirit took him.

Mrs O'Dea   You gave your good suit to a poor madman to be eaten?

Thomas   I was glad to give it to him. Though indeed truly, it was one of Harrison's suits, and the last of my finery from the old days. A nice civilian suit, made by Harrison, in North Great George's Street, years ago.

Mrs O'Dea   I can't believe that you gave away a suit like that. A lovely bespoke suit.

Thomas   Why not? Amn't I a lunatic myself?

Mrs O'Dea (*sensibly*)   Well, there must be a year's eating in a man's suit. You won't need to give him the new one.

Thomas   No, but it won't be much to me all the same, if it has no gold in it. The boy that sings to me betimes wears gold, and I have a hankering now for a suit with a touch of gold. There was never enough gold in that uniform. If I had made commissioner I might have had gold, but that wasn't a task for a Catholic, you understand, in the way of things, in those days.

Mrs O'Dea   You must have been a fine policeman, if they made you all of a chief superintendent.

Thomas   Maybe so. But, to tell you the truth, I was forty-five years in the DMP when they did so, and promotion was really a matter of service. Not that they would put a fool to such a task, when you think of the terrible responsibility of it. I had three hundred men in B Division, and kept all the great streets and squares of Dublin orderly and safe, and was proud, proud to do it well.

Mrs O'Dea   I am sure you did, Mr Dunne, because you carry yourself well yet. You mustn't mind Mr Smith. He's younger than yourself and one of his brothers was shot in the twenties, so he tells me.

Thomas   The DMP was never armed, not like the Royal Irish Constabulary. The RIC could go to war. That's why we were taken off the streets during that rebellion at Easter time, that they make so much of now. We were mostly country men, and Catholics to boot, and we loved our King and we loved our country. They never put those Black and Tans among us, because we were a force that belonged to Dublin and her streets. We did our best and followed our orders. Go out to Mount Jerome some day, in the city of Dublin, and see the old monument to the DMP men killed in the line of duty. Just ordinary country men keen to do well. And when the new government came in, they treated us badly. Our pensions were in disarray. Some said we had been traitors to Ireland. Though we sat in Dublin Castle all through twenty-two and tried to protect the city while the whole world was at each other's throats. While the most dreadful and heinous murders took place in the fields of Ireland. With nothing but our batons and our pride. Maybe we weren't much. You're thinking, of course he would speak well for his crowd. Yes, I'll speak well for them. We were part of a vanished world, and I don't know what's been put in our place. I'd like to see them clear Sackville Street of an illegal gathering without breaking a few heads. There was a proclamation posted the week before that meeting. It was my proper duty to clear the thoroughfare. There was no one killed that day that I know of, there were scores of my men in Jervis Street and the like, with head wounds. I'm sorry Smith's brother was killed. I'm sorry for all the poor souls killed these last years. Let them come and kill me if they wish. But I know my own story of what happened, and I am content with it.

Mrs O'Dea   Mercy, Mr Dunne, I didn't mean to prompt a declaration. You're all in a sweat, man. The sooner you have a new suit, the better.

Thomas   But I tell you, there's other things I regret, and I regret them sorely, things of my own doing, and damn history.

Mrs O'Dea   We all have our regrets, man dear. Do calm yourself.

Thomas   I regret that day with my daughter Annie and the sword, when we were home and snug in Kiltegan at last.

Mrs O'Dea   There, there, man dear. We'll see if we can't keep the next suit on you, when you go a-walking in the lunatics' meadow, as you call it. It's just the exercise field, you know, the walking meadow. It will have plenty of yellow in it.

Thomas   (*differently, head down*)   I suppose it is very sad about Patrick O'Brien. I suppose.

Mrs O'Dea   I have all your measurements now, Mr Dunne. And a fine big-boned gentleman you are. (*Looking at his bare feet.*) What became of your shoes, but?

Mrs O'Dea *and* **Thomas** (*after a moment, as one*)   Patrick O'Brien!

Mrs O'Dea   Maybe there's a pair of decent shoes about in the cupboards, that someone has left.

Thomas   Coffin shoes, you mean, I expect. Oh, I don't mind a dead man's shoes. And a nice suit, yes, that I can wear in my own coffin, to match, with yellow thread.

Mrs O'Dea   Not yet, Mr Dunne, not by a long chalk. (*Going out.*) I'll do my best for you. (*Locking the door.*)

Thomas (*alone, in an old summer light*)   When the rain of autumn started that year, my mother and me went down into the valley by the green road. Myself trotting beside her in my boyish joy. We passed the witch's farm, where the witch crossed the fields in her dirty dress to milk her bloodied cow, that gave her bloodied milk, a thing to fear because she used the same well as ourselves, and washed her bucket there before drawing water. My father was the steward of Humewood and she should have feared to hurt our well, but you cannot withstand the mad. Well, we passed the nodding bell-flowers that I delighted to burst, and ventured out on to the Baltinglass road, to beg a perch for our bums on a cart. (*Sitting up on the bedstead.*) For my father would not let my mother take the pony and trap, because he said the high lamps made too great a show of pride, and we were proud people enough without having to show it. Not that he didn't drive the trap himself when he needed. But we were soon in the old metropolis of Baltinglass, a place of size and wonder to a boy. (*Pulling out his ragged socks from under the mattress.*) There we purchased a pair of lace-up boots. A pair of lace-up boots which banished bare feet, which I was soon able to lace and tighten for myself of a morning, when the air in the bedroom was chill as a well, and the icy cock crowed in the frosty yard, and Thomas Dunne was young and mightily shod. (*Looking down at his feet.*) And Dolly my daughter later polished my policeman's boots, and Annie and Maud brought me my clothes brushed and starched in the mornings, as the castle of soldiers and constables woke.

When my poor wife was dead those many years, and Little
Ship Street stirred with the milkman's cart. And the sun
herself brought gold to the river's back. (*He looks at the locked
door.*) If they lock that door how can my daughters come to
rescue me? (*He holds out a hand and takes it with his other hand,
and shakes.*) How do you do? How do you do? (*Very pleased.*)
How do you do? (*Holds out his arms, embraces someone.*) How do
you do? (*Gently.*) How do you do? Oh, how do you do?

Music. After a little, **Smith** *enters with a cracked bowl with a steam
of stew off it. He hands* **Thomas** *a big spoon which* **Thomas** *holds
obediently.*

Smith   You look just like an old saint there, Mr Dunne, an
old saint there, with your spoon. You may think me a rough
sort of man but I know my saints. I seen a picture of St
Jerome with a spoon like that and a bowl like that. (**Thomas**
sits to eat.) Eat away, man. You should see the cauldron of
that stuff the cooks have made. The kitchens are in a fog.
Seven lambs went into it, they say. Isn't it good stuff?
(*Friendly.*) What's it your name is again, your first name? I've
so many to remember.

Thomas   Thomas. They named me Thomas long ago for
my great-great-grandfather the first steward of Humewood,
the big place in Kiltegan, the main concern. Though all his
own days they called him White Meg on account of his fierce
white beard. He'd stride up the old street from his house to
the great gates and say nothing to no one. White Meg. But
Thomas it was, was his name.

Smith   With your spoon. St Thomas! When I brought Mrs
O'Dea her cocoa in at five, she had you all cut out and hung
up on a hook with the other inhabitants, and the breeze was
blowing you softly from the crack in the pane. She's a keen
seamstress. St Thomas. Do you like the stew?

Thomas (*expansively*)   Of all the dishes in the world I may
say I relish mostly a stew.

Smith   You, St Thomas, that knew kings and broke Larkin.
Stew.

Thomas (*alerted*)   Put a piece of lamb in it at the bottom, for the men that are working, and let the child eat off the top of it. The child's spoon is a shallow spoon. Parsnips. The secret of stew on our hillside was just a scrape of crab apple in it – just a scrape. But then we'd fierce crab apples. And not to curse while it was cooking. And not to spit while it was cooling.

Smith   What was the name of the patriot was killed years past in Thomas Street outside the church of St Thomas, in the city of Dublin?

Thomas (*thinking, innocently*)   Thomas Street wasn't in my division. But Emmet, was it, you mean? Robert Emmet?

Smith   That's the one. They hung him there and the people cried out against the soldiers and the peelers, and after they dragged his body over the parade ground till it was bleeding and broken in its bones, and then they got a loyal butcher to cut him into four pieces. He was dead then.

Thomas   I should think.

Smith   That's what they did to him, those official men, and a fine Protestant gentleman at that.

Thomas (*pleasantly*)   It's as well to throw a bit of rosemary across it too, if you have rosemary. Rosemary smells good when the land gets hot. Across the stew. Rosemary. Thyme would do either, if you've none. When you put in the spuds. Or lavender maybe. Did you ever try clover? A child will eat clover when he is set down on the meadow to sit. The bee's favourite. A cow makes fine milk from a field of clover. So put in rosemary, if you have it. Ah, fresh spuds, turned out of the blessed earth like – for all the world like newborn pups. (*Laughing.*)

Smith   I suppose you held the day of Emmet's death as a festive day. A victory day. I suppose you did. I suppose you were all very queer indeed up there in the Castle. I'm thinking too of the days when they used to put the pitch caps on the priests when they catched them, like they were only dogs, and behind the thick walls of the city hall all the English fellas would be laughing at the screams of the priests, while their brains boiled. I'm thinking of all that. I suppose you never put a pitch cap on anyone. They weren't in fashion in your time. A pity. It must have been a great sight, all the same.

Thomas (*eating rapidly*)   Good stew, good stew. Wicklow lambs.

Smith (*looking at him*)   St Thomas, isn't it?

Thomas (*smiling*)   St Thomas.

Smith *goes off with the empty bowl.*

I loved her for as long as she lived, I loved her as much as I loved Cissy my wife, and maybe more, or differently. When she died it was difficult to go from her to the men that came after her, Edward and George, they were good men but it was not the same. When I was a young recruit it used to frighten me how much I loved her. Because she had built everything up and made it strong, and made it shipshape. The great world that she owned was shipshape as a ship. All the harbours of the earth were trim with their granite piers, the ships were shining and strong. The trains went sleekly through the fields, and her mark was everywhere, Ireland, Africa, the Canadas, every blessed place. And men like me were there to make everything peaceable, to keep order in her kingdoms. She was our pride. Among her emblems was the gold harp, the same harp we wore on our helmets. We were secure, as if for eternity the orderly milk-drays would come up the streets in the morning, and her influence would reach everywhere, like the salt sea pouring up into the fresh waters of the Liffey. Ireland was hers for eternity, order was everywhere, if we could but honour her example. She loved her Prince. I loved my wife. The world was a wedding of loyalty, of steward to Queen, she was the very flower and perfecter of Christendom. Even as the simple man I was I could love her fiercely. Victoria.

The **Recruit**, *a young man of eighteen or so comes on. He has obviously made a great effort to smarten himself for this meeting. He is tall and broad, and stoops a little as he takes off his hat.*

Good morning, son. How are you?

Recruit   Oh, most pleasant, sir, most pleasant.

Thomas   You had a good journey up from your home place?

Recruit   It didn't take a feather out of me, sir.

Thomas   Good man. What age are you?

Recruit   Eighteen, sir, this November past.

Thomas   Height?

Recruit   Six foot three, sir, in my winter socks.

Thomas   Well, you look a very fine man indeed. You were never in trouble yourself, son?

Recruit   Oh, no, sir.

Thomas   And did you serve in the Great War? I don't suppose you could have.

Recruit   No, sir. I was too young.

Thomas   Of course. A soldier doesn't always make a good policeman. There's too much – sorrow – in a soldier. You're a drinking man?

Recruit   I'll drink a glass of porter, with my father.

Thomas   Very good. I've read your father's letter. And I want to tell you, we are going to give you a go at it. I have a big book in my office within, bound in gold, that has the name of every DMP man that has ever served the crown. Do you wish for your own name to be added in due course?

Recruit   Oh – indeed and I do, sir. Most fervently.

Thomas   I hope you will do well, son. These are troubled times, and men like yourself are sorely needed. I will be watching your progress – watching, you understand, in a fatherly way. Do your best.

Recruit   I will, sir. Thank you, sir!

Thomas (*taking his hand*)   I was a young recruit myself once. I know what this means to you.

Recruit   The world, sir, it means the world.

Thomas   Good man. I'll write to your father in Longford. Take this now as a token of our good faith. (*Handing him the spoon.*)

Recruit   Thank you, sir, thank you.

*The **Recruit** shadows away. **Thomas** kneels at the end of his bed and grips the metal tightly.*

Thomas   I must not speak to shadows. When you see the shadows, Thomas, you must not speak. Sleep in the afternoon, that's the ticket. How did I get myself into this pickle, is it age just? I know I did what Annie said I did, but was it really me, and not some old disreputable creature that isn't me? When it was over, I knew suddenly in the car coming here what had happened, but at the time, at the time, I knew nothing, or I knew something else. And it was the gap between the two things that caused me to cry out in the car, the pain of it, the pain of it, the fright of it, and no one in the world to look at me again in a manner that would suggest that Thomas Dunne is still human, still himself. Everything is as clear as a glass. I can remember how lovely Cissy was the day we married, and that smile she gave me when the priest was finished, how she looked up at me in front of all our people, her face shining, astonishing me. You don't expect to see love like that. And that's a long time ago. And I can remember, now, the last day with Annie, and how I was feeling that day, and I can see myself there in the kitchen, and I know how mad I was. And I am ashamed. I am ashamed. I am ashamed. (*After a while of breathing like a runner.*) Hail Mary, full of Grace, the Lord is with thee, blessed art Thou amongst women, and blessed is the fruit of

thy womb. (*He gets stuck, bangs his head with his right palm.*) –
Jesus. Holy Mary, mother of. Holy Mary, mother of. I
remember, I do remember. Hail Mary full of grace the Lord
is with me blessed art Thou amongst women and blessed is
the fruit of Thy womb Jesus holy Mary Mother of . . . of . . .
of God! Of God! (*Climbs into bed.*) Robert Emmet. (*Pulls the
sheet over his face.*) Robert Emmet. (*Spits the t's so the sheet blows
up from his lips.*) Robert Emmet. (*After a moment.*) Sleep, sleep,
that's the ticket.

His son, **Willie**, *neat and round, comes in and sits on the end of his
bed and sings to him Schubert's* Ave Maria. *At the end,* **Thomas**
looks over the sheet. **Willie** *wears his army uniform.*

Hello, child. Are you warm?

Willie   It's cold in the mud, Father.

Thomas   I know child. I'm so sorry.

Sunlight grows slowly over the scene, banishing **Willie**. *The imagined
stir and calling of the Castle below.* **Thomas** *is at ease suddenly. His
middle daughter,* **Annie**, *in a light cotton dress of the early twenties,
a bow in her spine, carries on a white shirt, which illumines like a
lantern when she crosses the windowlight. There's an old music.*

Annie   Now, Papa – there's the best-ironed shirt in
Christendom.

Thomas   Thank you, dear.

Annie   It took the best part of an hour to heat the hearth,
to heat the iron. There's enough starch in the breast to
bolster Jericho.

Thomas   Thank you, dear.

Annie   If Dolly had ironed it, you'd look at it more intently.

Thomas   I am looking at it, Annie. Or I would, if it weren't
so blinding white.

Annie   And it isn't that white, Papa. And you've things on
your mind today, I know. A black day.

Thomas   I expect it is.

Annie   Why Collins of all people to give the Castle to? Couldn't they find a gentleman?

Thomas   He is the head of the new government, Annie.

Annie   Government! We know what sort of men they are. Coming in here to the likes of you. Whose son gave his life for Ireland.

Thomas (*coming over to her, kindly*)   Will gave his life to save Europe, Annie, which isn't the same thing.

Annie   I miss Willie, Papa. I miss him. We need him today.

Thomas   I blame myself. There was no need for him to go off, except, he hadn't the height to be a policeman. The army were glad to take him. I blame myself.

Annie   Will was proud, Papa, proud to be in the Rifles. It was his life.

Thomas   It was the death of him. You cannot lose a son without blaming yourself. But that's all history now. Annie.

Maud, *his eldest, a very plain woman with black hair, dressed heavily for the bright day, carries on his dress uniform, struggling to balance the ceremonial sword.*

Let me help you.

Maud   It's all right, Papa, I'll plonk it on the bed.

Thomas   Where's Dolly?

Maud   Polishing the boots. I hate to see a woman spit. Lord, Lord, she's a spitter, when it's Papa's old shoes. And she was away out this morning, I know not why, all secretive.

Annie   Away out this morning? She didn't touch her bed all night. Up at that dance at the Rotunda. She should be whipped.

Maud   And did you say she could go to that dance?

Annie   I didn't say she could take all night to walk home.

Thomas   Thoughtful daughters you are, to be helping me so. How did you get the creases so firm?

Maud   I slept on them. In as much as I slept. I cannot sleep these times.

Thomas   I could meet the emperor of the world with those creases.

Annie   You'll have to make do with Michael Collins.

Maud   Oh, don't start that old story, Annie. We've had enough of it now, God knows.

Annie   I was only saying.

Maud   Well, don't be only saying. Go and stir the teapot, can't you, and give over the politics.

Annie   I was only saying.

Maud   You're only always only saying, and you have me stark wide-eyed in the bed all night, worrying and turning and fretting, and a great headache pounding away, because you can leave nothing alone, Annie, till you have us all miserable and mad with concern.

Thomas   Now, girls, think of your mother. Would she want you to be talking like this?

Maud   No, Papa, of course not. She would not.

Annie   Mam? What do you know about Mam, if I may ask?

Maud   Don't I see her often when I sleep? Don't I see her blue polka-dot dress, yes, and her bending down to me and making me laugh?

Annie   That's only ould stuff Willie told us.

Maud   Oh, Annie, Annie, I was four years old, you were only two!

Thomas   Daughters, daughters – what a terrible thing to be arguing about!

Annie   Oh, a thing indeed.

Maud (*after a little*)   I'm sorry, Annie.

Annie   That's all right, girl. It's not your fault Collins is a criminal.

Maud   I'll be dead, that's it! I'll be dead by day's end. I can't take everything in! My head's bursting with Papa and Michael Collins and I don't know what . . .

Dolly, *holding out the polished boots carefully from her dress, starts across to* **Thomas**, *smiling.* **Thomas**'*s face lights like a lamp.*

Thomas   Oh, Dolly, Dolly, Dolly!

Before she reaches him, an intrusion of darkness, the scattering of his daughters. **Thomas** *roars, with pain and confusion. He lifts his arms and roars. He beats the bed. He hits the table. He roars.* **Smith** *unlocks the door and hurries in, brandishing a pacifier. It looks like a baton.*

Smith   What the hell is all the shouting? You have the pauper lunatics in a swelter! Crying and banging their heads, and laughing like fairground mechanicals, and spitting, and cutting themselves with items. (*Looking back out.*) Mrs O'Dea, Mrs O'Dea – try and sort those screamers!

Mrs O'Dea (*off*)   I will, I will!

Smith   Even the long ward of old dames with their dead brains, have some of them opened their eyes and are weeping to be woken, with your bloody shouting. Do you want to go in with them, old man? After I beat you!

Thomas (*hurrying back into his bed*)   I only shouted the one time. It must have been the moon woke them. (*Drawing the sheet high.*) My daughter Annie gives you the shillings for the room, Black Jim.

Smith   She can give all the shillings she likes. She won't know where we throw you.

Thomas Don't put Thomas with the poor dribblers. I've seen them. I've seen that terrible long ward of women, belonging to no one at all, no one to pay shillings for them. Don't put me there.

Smith Then show me silence. (*Striking the end of the bed.*)

Thomas Don't strike there. My son sits there.

Smith You are a violent, stupid man, Mr Dunne, and I want silence out of you!

Thomas (*a finger to his lips*) Silence.

Smith *goes, banging the door, locking it harshly.*

(*Pulling up the sheet.*) Robert Emmet.

Annie *has slipped over to his bed.*

Annie Papa.

Thomas (*looking out again*) I must be silent, child.

Annie Papa, please will you tell me.

Thomas What, child?

Annie Why is my back bowed, Papa?

Thomas Why, child, because of your polio.

Annie Why, Papa?

Thomas I don't know, Annie. Because it afflicts some and leaves others clear. I don't know.

Annie Will I ever have a husband, Papa?

Thomas I do hope so.

Annie I think a woman with such a back will not find a husband.

Thomas She might.

Annie I see the prams going by in Stephen's Green, glistening big prams, and I look in when the nannies are polite, and I look in, and I see the babies, with their round

faces, and their smells of milk and clean linen, and their
heat, and Papa –

Thomas Yes, child?

Annie They all look like my babies.

Annie *goes,* **Thomas** *looks after her, then covers his face again. A
country music. He sleeps, he sleeps. The moon, the emblem of lunacy,
appears overhead, pauses there faintly, fades again. It is a very
delicate, strange sleep. The calling of a cock distantly, birdsong, the
cock louder. An arm of sunlight creeps into the room and across*
Thomas'*s covered face. His hand creeps out and his fingers wave in
the light. He pulls down the sheet and the noises cease. He listens.
Imitates the cock softly.*

Thomas The cock crows in the morning yard, banishing all
night fears. No person, that has not woken to the crowing of
a familiar cock, can know how tender that cry is evermore,
stirring the child out into the fresh fingers of sunlight, into
the ever-widening armfuls of sunlight. How stray the child
looks in the yard, bare feet on the old pack-stones in the clay,
all his people have come out in their own vanished times, as
small as him, surrounded by the quiet byres just wakening
now, the noses of the calves wet in the closed dark, the sitting
hens in the coop anxious to be released, out away from the
night fear of foxes, so they may lay their eggs beyond finding
in the hayshed and the hawthorn bushes. Only the boy
knows their terrible tricks. He inserts an arm into the known
places and feels the warm eggs, smells them happily in his
brown palms, and searches out the newest places of the hens
in the deepest bowers of the straw. He carries them back in
to his Ma Ma, folded in his gansey, with the glow of pride
about him as big as the sun. Then he goes back out into the
yard while the eggs are boiling, or put aside carefully for the
cake, and tries to read the story of the day in the huge pages
of the clouds. And he sees the milking cow driven up on to
the top field where the summer grass is rich and moist, and
how well he knows the wild garden there of meadowsweet,
where the dragonfly is hard as pencil. And the boy's Ma Ma

is calling him, and he goes, and there is no greater morning, no morning in his life of greater importance.

Smith *enters with a newspaper. He fetches out* **Thomas**'s *po. It's empty.*

Smith   I hope you're not blocking up like some of the old fellows.

Thomas   A deserted house needs no gutter. Is that my newspaper?

Smith   It is. (*Throws it to him.* **Thomas** *opens it.*) Can you not order a decent newspaper?

Thomas   *Irish Times* suits me.

Smith   It's all fools on horseback.

Thomas   Not so much. I'm trying to keep up on the activities, if I may call them that, of a certain Hinky Dink Kenna, who runs the first ward in Chicago. I tell you, you'd have to call him a criminal here. Himself and Bath-house John Coughlan. Villains. If they had never left Ireland, I'd have had to lock them up in Mountjoy. But you can do what you like in America, or so it seems.

Smith   Is that right? And what do they get up to, those two?

Thomas   Oh, they're in the liquor trade, you might say. It makes powerful reading.

Mrs O'Dea *comes in with big flaps of black cloth –* **Thomas**'s *suit in its unsewn parts.*

Smith   He hasn't washed himself.

Mrs O'Dea   Didn't you wash him yesterday? Do you want to rub him out? Come on up, Mr Dunne, and let me pin these to you for a look at it.

Smith   Can't you see he's reading.

Thomas (*getting out of bed*)   Oh, I've time for reading. In my retirement.

He stands for the fitting. **Mrs O'Dea** *begins to pin the sections of the suit to his long johns.*

Mrs O'Dea   You're the cleanest man in Baltinglass.

Thomas *seems agitated, looking down at the sections.*

What's the matter, Mr Dunne?

Thomas   That's just the old black stuff.

Mrs O'Dea   And what if it is?

Thomas (*so* **Smith** *won't hear*) Didn't we discuss yellow?

Mrs O'Dea   Yellow thread, Mr Dunne. I can only stitch the sections together with yellow. The trustees buy us in the black cloth from Antrim.

Thomas   But it's fierce, foul stuff, isn't it?

Smith   I'll leave you to it, Mrs O'Dea. I'll be over in the Monkey Ward, sluicing them out, if you need me. Be good, Mr Dunne. (*Goes.*)

Mrs O'Dea (*taking a bobbin from her apron*)   Look it, isn't that the bee's knees? That's from my own sewing box, that Mr O'Dea gave me in the old days. I can't do fairer than that.

Thomas   Oh, it's very sunny.

Mrs O'Dea   Now. (*Pinning again.*) It'll do beautifully. Can't your daughter bring you in clothes, if you don't like mine?

Thomas   I wouldn't go bothering her. All my daughters are good, considerate women. We looked after each other, in that fled time, when their mother was dead.

Mrs O'Dea   I'm sorry, Mr Dunne. And how did she die?

Thomas   They never failed their father, their Papa, in that fled time. You should have seen them when they were little. Three little terrors going round with the knicks to their knees.

Mrs O'Dea (*pricking him by mistake*)   Oh, sorry. And where are your other daughters, Mr Dunne, these days?

Thomas We stood under the hawthorn, while the bees broke their hearts at the bell-flowers, because the fringes of darkness had closed them.

Mrs O'Dea Who did, Mr Dunne?

Thomas My wife Cissy and myself. Cecilia. In courting days. Old courting days.

Mrs O'Dea And what did she die of, did you say? (*Pricking.*)

Thomas Nothing at all. Her farm was Lathaleer, her father's farm. The most beautiful piece of land. He was woodsman and keeper at Humewood, but he was a most dexterous farmer. The Cullens of Lathaleer. What a match she was for me! A strong, straight-backed, sensible person that loved old steps and tunes. She'd rather learn a new step than boil turnips, old Cullen said to me – but it wasn't so. What does a father know? King Edward himself praised her hair, when we were presented in nineteen-three. A thorough mole-black devious hair she had.

Mrs O'Dea I'm sure. And didn't you do well by her, rising so high, and everything?

Thomas Our happiest days were when I was only an inspector in Dalkey village. We lived there in a house called Polly Villa. There was precious little villainy in Dalkey. Three girls she bore there, three girls. And the boy already, before we came.

Mrs O'Dea You have a son too? You have a lot.

Thomas No. No, he didn't come back from France that time. He wrote me a lovely letter.

Mrs O'Dea (*after a little*) And King Edward praised your wife's hair. Fancy.

Thomas Aye – All the ladies loved him. Of course, he was old in that time. But a true king.

Mrs O'Dea (*finished with the fitting, unpinning him again*)   What would you say about King De Valera?

Thomas   I would say very little about him, in that I wouldn't know much to say. Of course, I see a bit about him in the papers.

Mrs O'Dea   As much a foreigner as the King of England ever was, Mr O'Dea used to say, when he was overground. Mr O'Dea was a pundit, I'm afraid.

Thomas   He wants to buy the Irish ports back from Mr Churchill. I think that's a great pity. A man that loves his King might still have gone to live in Crosshaven or Cobh, and called himself loyal and true. But soon there'll be nowhere in Ireland where such hearts may rest.

Mrs O'Dea   You're as well to keep up with the news, Mr Dunne.

Thomas   I had an admiration for the other man though, the general that was shot, I forget his name.

Mrs O'Dea (*ready to go*)   Who was that?

Thomas   I forget. I remember the shock of sorrow when he was killed. I remember Annie and me crying in the old parlour of our quarters in the Castle. A curiosity. I met him, you see, the one time. He was very courteous and praised Wicklow and said a few things to me that rather eased my heart, at the time. But they shot him.

Mrs O'Dea (*going*)   They shot a lot of people. Was it Collins?

Thomas   I don't know, I forget. I remember the sorrow but not the name. Maybe that was the name.

Mrs O'Dea   I may have left a few pins in you, Mr Dunne, so don't go dancing about unduly.

Thomas   Dancing? I never danced in my life. I was a tree at a dance.

Mrs O'Dea *goes off.* **Thomas** *discovers a pin and holds it up.*

Where are your other daughters, Mr Dunne, these days? (*After a little, moving the pin about like a tiny sword.*) The barracks of Ireland filled with new faces. And all the proud regiments gone, the Dublin Rifles and the Dublin Fusiliers. All the lovely uniforms. All the long traditions, broken up and flung out, like so many morning eggs on to the dung heap. Where are your other daughters, Mr Dunne, these days? Dolly of the hats. Annie told me the name of the place. Somewhere in America. What was the name?

The light of their parlour in the Castle. **Annie** *comes on with a big bundle of socks to sort. She sits on the three-legged stool. The socks are all the same. She looks in the socks for holes by thrusting her right hand into each of them, sorts the good from the bad.*

Annie   There's a terrible queer sort of a quietness settled over this Castle. How Papa expects to hang on here now till September. The city will be rubble, rubble by September.

Maud *follows on looking pale and alarmed.*

Maud   Have you seen that Dolly?

Annie   No.

Maud   I can't keep a hoult on her at all these days.

Annie   She'll be down the town, as usual.

Maud   How can she go shopping in times like these?

Annie   What's civil unrest to Dolly and her shopping?

Maud (*feeling the back of her head*)   Oh, dear.

Annie   What is it, Maud?

Maud   Nothing, nothing at all.

Annie   Maud, what is it now?

Maud   I have an ache here, Annie, at the base of the skull, do you think it might be something deadly?

Annie   I never knew a one to worry like you do, girl.

Maud   Do you want to feel it? Is there a lump?

Annie Don't come near me with your head! It's nothing. It's called a headache. Any normal person would accept that it's a headache. Girl, sometimes I don't wonder if you mightn't be seriously astray in your wits, girl.

Maud Oh, don't say that, Annie.

Annie Am I not allowed sort the darning in peace?

Dolly *comes in to them, wearing a neat outfit. She looks subdued.*

What's happened you, Dolly?

Maud I was all over the yards looking for you, Dolly, where on earth do you get to, these days?

Dolly I was down at the North Wall with the Galligan sisters.

Maud At the North Wall?

Annie What were you doing there, Dolly?

Dolly Mary Galligan was going out with one of the Tommies, and he and his troop were heading off home today, so we went down to see them off.

Annie (*sorting away*) Well, well, I don't know, Dolly, if you aren't the biggest fool in Christendom.

Dolly No, I'm no fool. They were nice lads. There was a good crowd down there, and the Tommies were in high spirits, singing and so on. It was very joyful.

Maud You've to keep your skirts long these times, Dolly. You're not to be seen waving to soldiers.

Dolly They're going from Ireland and they'll never be back, why shouldn't we say goodbye? Do you know every barracks in Ireland has lost its officers and men? Regiments that protected us in the war, who went out and left thousands behind in France. Willie's own regiment is to be disbanded, and that's almost entirely Dublin lads.

Annie Dolly, why are you so surprised? Haven't we known for the last six months that Ireland is to be destroyed? I

don't know why it's such news to you. Haven't you listened?
Haven't you seen your father's face? Haven't you felt for him,
Dolly?

Dolly   It's different when you see it.

Annie   You're a fool, Dolly.

Dolly   I'm no fool.

Annie *picks up in one hand the good socks and in the other the ones
needing mending – they look like two woolly hands themselves.*

And I'll tell you. Coming home in the tram, up the docks
road, Mary Galligan was crying, and we were talking kindly
to her, and trying to comfort her, and I don't know what we
said exactly, but this woman, a middle-aged woman, quite
well-to-do, she rises up and stands beside us like a long
streak of misery, staring at us. And she struck Mary Galligan
on the cheek, so as she left the marks of her hand there. And
she would have attacked me too, but that the conductor
came down and spoke to the woman. And she said we were
Jezebels and should have our heads shaved and be whipped,
for following the Tommies. And the conductor looked at her,
and hadn't he served in France himself, as one of the
Volunteers, oh, it was painful, the way she looked back at
him, as if he were a viper, or a traitor. The depth of
foolishness in her. A man that had risked himself, like Willie,
but that had reached home at last.

Dolly *crying.* **Annie** *gets up and puts her arms around her, still
holding the socks.*

Annie   Things will sort themselves out, Dolly dear.

Dolly   If she had shot us it wouldn't have been so bad.

Annie   Things will sort themselves out.

Maud *feeling the back of her head again, confused.*

We'll put on our aprons and get the tea. We'll go on
ourselves as if we were living in paradise. (*The three go out.*)

Thomas   Their father's face. Their father's face.

He puts his hands over his face. **Matt**, *a youngish man in a hat, his shirt sleeves held by metal circlets, sets up his easel centrestage. Sunlight gathers about him, clearing the sense of* **Thomas**'s *room. Rooks. A suggestion of meadow grass.* **Matt** *holds a square of cut-out cardboard to the view, deciding on a composition. He wipes at his face.*

Matt   Midges! The artist's bane!

Thomas *approaches him, a little wildly.*

Thomas   Patrick O'Brien, Patrick O'Brien, wherever did you bury my suit, man dear? They are tormenting me with dark cloth, and I hope you will give it back to me, despite your great prowess and fame, as a bulleter.

Matt   It isn't who you think, Thomas. It is Matt Kirwin that married your daughter Maud.

Thomas (*astonished*)   Oh – is it? (*After a moment.*) You have a strong look of Patrick about you. Except I see now, you are not on all fours, as I would expect. Are you a hero too?

Matt (*kindly*)   How are you getting on, Thomas?

Thomas   How does it come that you are here in the walking meadow? I only ask, as I am used to seeing people hither and thither and yon. (*Feeling his arms for solidity.*) Have you lost your wits also?

Matt   Maybe so, but I have brought Annie over in the Ford. We're over there in Kiltegan for a week or two with the little boys. I thought I might capture a water-colour while I waited.

Thomas   You might, like a man might capture a butterfly. You haven't started your capturing.

Matt   In a minute, when I decide the view I want. The painting itself will only take a moment.

Thomas   They're all choice views. Where's Maud then?

Matt   She stayed in Dublin this time.

Thomas   It isn't the melancholy?

Matt I don't know what it is. She has certainly kept to her bed of recent months. Has she been right since the second boy came? I don't know.

Thomas Her mother was always very jolly. I don't know where she gets it from.

Matt The sea air of Howth will cure all that, in time, the sea air, the quieter nature of life there in Howth, and the boys. She does love to see the boys, and they are most dignified and splendid boys.

Thomas You say? (*Warmly.*) Well, Matt (*taking* **Matt**'s *hand*), how are you? (*Oddly.*) How do you do?

Matt We're going along fine. I'm teaching in the technical school in Irishtown – for my sins. And painting for myself when I can. I have done a great deal of work on the Great South Wall, in my lunchtimes. The Poolbeg Lighthouse? But we couldn't get by at all without Annie. She keeps everything going.

Thomas Yes, yes, she told me you had one of your drawings printed up in a book, didn't you, yes, of the Bailey Lighthouse I think she said. You will be a great expert soon on lighthouses.

Matt (*pleased*) It was little enough.

Thomas Ah, Matthew, it is good to see you. You're looking so well. I forget, you know, I forget how much I like you. And the boys, the two grand boys, will I see them today? Are they in the Ford?

Matt No, Thomas. They're so little still, and this is such a strange spot, for children, and, you know, they were a bit upset the last time. The elder boy has read his *Oliver Twist* and you were all mixed up in his mind with Fagan. Do you remember, at the end of the book, when the child is brought in to see Fagan before Fagan is hanged?

Thomas Hanged? No.

Matt Maud was worried that . . .

Thomas   Certainly, certainly. You must excuse my long
johns. I lost my suit only recently. As a matter of fact, it
must be buried around here somewhere. Well, no matter,
they'll make me another, and then maybe you will bring my
grandsons again to see me? Or you could fetch me over to
Kiltegan in the Ford if they were afraid of this place. I'd be
very quiet for you in the Ford.

Matt   Of course, Thomas.

Thomas   I know I look a sight. And that won't do for such
fine boys. I only saw them those few times, but, I think it is
the smell of children that gets in upon you. You long for it
then. And the roundness of them, and the love they show
you. It could be anywhere about here, my suit. But I'm
having a touch of gold put into the new one – well, yellow,
anyhow.

Matt   You'll find Annie in your room if you go up, I'll be
bound. She thought you were inside, you know.

Thomas   Yellow thread, you know?

Matt   All right.

Thomas   Matt, I don't like to ask Annie, to bother her, but
do you think there's any great likelihood of my getting away
from here at all in the coming times?

Matt   I don't know rightly, Thomas.

Thomas   Of course, of course. It is quite a pleasant station.
You see all the country air we have. Not like the city. The
city would ruin a man's health. Though it has its beauties.
Do you know, I used at one time to be a policeman? Do you
know I used at one time be Chief Superintendent of B
Division? With responsibility for the Castle herself? It was I
cleared all the vermin out of Yorke Street, that time, the
fancy men from the Curragh and all their girls – it *was* me,
wasn't it, Matt? I held that post? You must bring the boys to
Kiltegan as often as you can.

Matt   Well, we do, Thomas. You have a fine vista here, look. (*Having him look into the cardboard framer.*) You do, what with those oaks, and the field of wheat beyond.

Thomas (*peering, after a moment*)   It's only grass just.

Matt   Oh, is it grass?

Thomas   Paint away, Matthew.

Matt   Thank you.

The light of **Thomas**'s *room again finds* **Annie**, *more spinsterish now, strong, bony, simply dressed, with her handbag and a brown paper bag. She looks anxious.* **Thomas** *goes to her with a great smile, raising his arms.*

Thomas (*searching in his mind for her name*)   Dolly – Maud – Annie!

Annie   Papa.

Thomas (*his arms collapsing slowly*)   What has happened to you, Annie? You look very different to how you were just this morning.

Annie   What happened to your clothes, Papa?

Thomas   I don't know, Dolly.

Annie   Annie, it is.

Thomas   Annie. I don't know. I think I heard there was a bit of thievery going on, but I don't think there's any truth in it. Nothing for the magistrate. I'll deal with it. You know Mr Collins is to take over the Castle in January. I'll need all my clothes done over like new.

Annie   No, Papa. That was all years ago. In bygone times. You are in Baltinglass County Home, Papa.

Thomas   I know. And I tell myself, so I won't forget. I had it written down somewhere, but I lost the bit of paper. What is it about the old head? Give me the name of any street in Dublin and I'll name every lane, alleyway, road, terrace and street around it. I could knit you the whole thing with names, and if you forgot a few places, and found a hole there in your memory, I could darn it for you. I am in effect a sort of Dublin Street Directory. But when it comes to the brass tacks of things, everyday matters, as, for instance, where in the name of God I am, well, daughter dear, I'm not so quick then. But look, girl, what Annie gave me. (*Going to his mattress and fetching a book out.*) A wonderful strange story about a boy on the Mississippi. And his friend. They are lost in a cave together, the two boys, and the poor bit of a greasy candle they have is burning lower and lower, and the demons of the dark are surely approaching . . . I feel I know that cave. Do you see, Dolly? I can see it when I put my hands over my face. Like this. Yes, there she is, the mighty Mississippi, going along like Godly pewter. And those poor boys, Huckleberry and Tom, and the yellow walls of the cave, and the big drips of water. Oh, Dolly, and the old granite bathing place at Vico Rock. And there's the terrible suck-up of water when Davy Barnes the newspaper vendor takes his dive, the fattest man in Ireland, and there's Annie, all decked out in her first communion regalia like a princess, oh, mercy, and there's the moon over a bay that reputable people have compared to Naples – Sorrento, Vico, beautiful Italian names living the life of Reilly in old Killiney and Dalkey. On a summer's night, you were born, Dolly, deep in the fresh dark, just when the need for candles failed. Oh, Dolly.

Annie (*trying to calm him*)   I gave you the book about the Mississippi, Papa. It's a book you loved in your youth, so you always said.

Thomas (*gripping her arm a bit roughly*)   Where is Maud, where is she, that she doesn't come in to me?

Annie   She's taken refuge, taken refuge you might say, in her own difficulties.

Thomas   Is that right? And Dolly, where is Dolly?

Annie   Gone out into the wide world, Papa. Would you blame her?

Thomas   Blame her? (*Formal again.*) How do you do? How is Maud? How are the boys? No, no, I know all that. Don't tell me. I won't waste your time, never you fear. How are you? That's the important thing to establish. That's how people go on among themselves, family people. Is there any word from Dolly in America? Annie, Annie, where is she in America?

Annie   Ohio, Papa?

Thomas   Ohio, Ohio! That's the place. Ah, I was tormented trying to think of the word. Ohio. Dolly in Ohio. I must write it down. Do you have a dragonfly – a pencil?

Annie   No, Papa, I don't. This room is so bare and dark, for all the shillings I give them. I hope they give you your paper. It's all I can manage, Papa, out of your pension. It is a very miserly pension. Matt makes up the rest of it for us. And he has a pittance.

Thomas   Don't I have a beautiful pension for my forty-five years of service?

Annie   No, Papa, you don't.

Thomas   I think I should have.

Annie   Look, Papa, what I brought for you. (*She pulls a bunch of heather from the bag.*)

Thomas   Oh, Lord, Lord. (*Smelling it in his hands tenderly.*) From the hills above Kiltegan. How the heat of the day makes the heather raise its smell to the grateful native. The peace, the deep peace in the evening as we stared, you and me, into the last lingering flames running across the ashen turf, and the ghostly tiredness in us after slaving about the place all day.

Annie   When was that, Papa?

Thomas   Those three years in Kiltegan, Annie, when you and me were left to amuse ourselves as we could, Annie. You remember?

Annie   I do, Papa, I remember the three years well enough. With you sinking lower and lower in your chair beside that fire, and muttering about this and that, and the way you had been abandoned, you wouldn't treat a dog like that, you said, muttering, muttering, till I was driven mad. And all the work of the dairy and the byre and the hens to do. It was like living with Hannibal in Abyssinia, when Hannibal was a leader no more.

Thomas   Who? Where? But didn't the Cullens of Lathaleer come visiting like royalty in their high trap, and the Dunnes of Feddin, and the Cullens of Kelsha?

Annie   No, Papa, they did not, not after you drove them away with insult and passing remarks.

Thomas   I never did. We lived there like, like . . .

Annie   Like, like the dead, Papa.

Thomas   (*angry*)   All right. So there were demons in the high wood, and the screams of the lost from the byres, and the foul eggs in the rotting hay, and every pitchfork in the barn was sharp, glinting sharp, for you to thrust into my breast.

Annie   Papa, Papa, calm and ease, calm and ease.

Thomas   Oh, fearsome, fearsome, fearsome. Can I see my grandsons?

Annie   (*holding on to her father*)   Papa, Papa. Your grandsons are afraid of you.

Thomas   Afraid? Filthy, filthy.

Annie   Papa, Papa. How many miles to Babylon?

Thomas   (*smiling*)   Babylon.

Annie   Three score and ten. Remember, Papa, remember?

Thomas   Will I be there by candlelight?

Annie   Sure, and back again.

Thomas   Candlelight. Oh, yes, yes. (*Weeping.*) Yes. (*Smiling.*) Yes.

Annie   How many times in that last year in Kiltegan did I have to sing you the songs to calm your fears?

Thomas   Was it so many?

Annie   Many, many, many. Three score and ten, Papa.

Thomas (*after a long breath*)   My father was the steward of Humewood, and I was the steward of Christendom. Look at me.

Annie   Papa, we've all to grow old.

Thomas (*patting her back with his right hand, like a child*)   Oh, yes. Oh, yes.

Annie *goes quietly.* **Thomas** *sits on the stool slowly. The door ajar.*

Candlelight. (*After a little.*) A bit of starch for a new shirt, a bit of spit for my shoes, I could set out for Kiltegan as an ordinary man and see those shining boys. (*After a little.*) No. (*After a little.*) And take them up and smell their hair and kiss their noses and make them do that laughter they have in them. (*After a little.*) No. (*After a little.*) Dear Lord, put the recruits back in their barracks in Fitzgibbon Street, put the stout hearts back into Christendom's Castle, and troop the colours once more for Princess and Prince, for Queen and for King, for Chief Secretary and Lord Lieutenant, for Viceroy and Commander-in-Chief. (*After a little.*) But you cannot. (*After a little.*) Put the song back in the mouth of the beggar, the tune back in the pennywhistle, the rat-tat-tat of the tattoo back in the parade ground, stirring up our hearts. (*After a little.*) But you cannot. (*After a little.*) – Gone. The hearth of Kiltegan. How many miles to Kiltegan, Nineveh and Babylon? The sun amiable in the yard and the moon in the oaks after darkness. The rabbitman stepping out of the woods at dusk with a stick of dangling snags and a dark greeting. – Gone. (*After a little, quietly.*) Candlelight. I walked out through the grounds of Loreto College as far as the sea. The midwife had bade me go. I was a man of fifty.

Rhododendrons. All night she had strained in the bed, she
was like a person pinned by a fallen rock, waving her arms
and legs and groaning, and shouting. Her shouts escaped
from Polly Villa and ran up the road to the station and down
the road to the village in darkness. I was becoming distressed
myself, so the midwife bade me go. Willie, Maud and Annie
had been difficult for her too, because she was small, small
and thin and hard-working. Cullen's daughter. And she was
like a sort of dancer in the bed, but stuck in the dance. King
Edward himself praised her hair, it was mole-black, though
there are no moles in Ireland. Out at sea, the lighthouse was
hard at work too, warning the mail-packet and the night
fishermen. I thought of all the nuns asleep up in the college,
asleep in their quiet rooms, the sea asleep herself at the foot
of the cliff. And I thought, I would do anything for that
woman of mine behind me in the house, where we had done
all our talking and laughing and our quarrelling. But my
mind was in a peculiar state. I thought of all the Sunday
roasts she had made, all piled up somewhere in eternity, a
measure of her expertise. And I thought of how much her
daughters and her son loved her, and depended on her for
every sort of information, and how stupid and silent I was
with my son. How she made the world possible and hopeful
for him and the two girls. (*Sits on bed.*) I started to tremble, it
was a moment in your life when daily things pass away from
you, when all your concerns seem to vanish, and you are
allowed by God a little space of clarity and grace. When you
see that God himself is in your wife and in your children, and
they hold in trust for you your own measure of goodness.
And in the manner of your treatment of them lies your own
salvation. I went back to the house with a lighter heart, a
simpler man than the one who had set out. And the house
was quiet. It was as if it were itself asleep, the very bricks,
living and asleep with a quiet heartbeat. (*Holding the pillow.*)
Suddenly I was terribly afeared that my new child was dead,
I don't know why. You expect its cries, you long for its cries.
I pushed open my front door and hurried down into the back
room. The midwife was over by the window, with a little
bundle. And Cissy was lying quiet, still, at ease. The midwife

came over immediately and placed her bundle in my arms. It was like holding a three-pound bag of loose corn. (*The pillow.*) And there was a little face in the midst of the linen, a little wrinkled face, with red skin, and two big round eyes seeming to look up at me. I pledged all my heart and life to that face, all my blood and strength to that face, all the usefulness of my days to that face. And that was Dolly. And that was just as the need for candlelight fails, and the early riser needs no candle for his task.

Music. Dark after a few moments.

Act Two

*Thomas's room as before, **Maud** holding his sword in readiness.
Annie near. **Dolly** looking at **Thomas** with the polished shoes just
on. He wears his dress uniform, the helmet as yet on the table.*

Thomas   Oh, Dolly, Dolly, Dolly.

Dolly   Will they do, Papa?

Thomas   They're beautiful shoes now.

Dolly   This whole day reminds me of when I was twelve,
and there were snipers on the roofs above the music-hall, and
me and Annie and Maud would be crawling along the
sandbags outside the gates, trying to get in home from the
shops. And laughing. And the soldiers at the gates laughing
too.

Annie   That poor lieutenant didn't laugh when they put a
bullet in his head.

Maud   And you were only ten then, Miss Dolly, and as wild
as a tenement cat.

Dolly   Will it be like that today?

Thomas   No, sweet, that's all done with now. This is an act
of peace.

Annie   My foot.

Thomas (*putting an arm about* **Dolly**)   Mr Collins and a small
staff will come in, and we'll all meet like gentlemen.

Annie   Ha.

Thomas   And he will take command of the place, in effect.
Don't you worry, Dolly, don't you worry.

Dolly   And what time is the meeting, Papa?

Thomas   Shortly. The chief secretary wanted to meet at six but Collins sent in a note to say he wasn't a blackbird.

Annie   Blackguard more like.

Dolly   You are sure no one will try to shoot you?

Thomas   Why would they want to shoot me?

Annie   They would hardly have offered Papa a position in their new police force if they wanted to shoot him.

Dolly   Did they, Papa? Oh, and will you take up that offer, Papa? It would be exciting.

Thomas   We'll be Wicklow people again by year's end. Look at your father, Dolly. I am sixty-six years old! I am too old for new things. Indeed, I wish I were a younger man again, and I could kiss your noses, like when you were babies, and make you scream with delight.

Maud   Papa! Come along, Papa, and we'll get your sword on you.

Maud *and* **Annie** *attach the sword to its belt.*

Thomas   A man with three such daughters, three beautiful daughters, will never be entirely worthless. This January morning is the start of peace, and we may enjoy that peace till September, and then be gone – gone like shadows of an old dispensation.

Dolly   A girl of eighteen is never a shadow, Papa.

Thomas   Today is – what do you call it – symbolical. (**Maud** *doing the last buttons on the jacket.*) Like those banners in the Chapel Royal for every lord lieutenant that has ruled Ireland. It's a mighty symbolical sort of a day, after all these dark years. I'll be worn out. I'll be practising now. (*Taking* **Dolly**'s *hand.*) Good man, Joe, good man, Harry – that's the constables, because they're young too, Dolly, and will be greatly affected. Oh, big country hands, with rural grips! I'll have crushed fingers, like a visiting king.

Annie   And well, Papa, you are a king, more than some of those other scallywags.

Thomas   That is the whole crux of the matter. I am not a king. I am the servant of a king. I am only one of the stewards of his Irish city.

Annie   Collins is no king either, begging your pardon. With a tally of carnage, intrigue and disloyalty that would shame a tinker. And that King, for all his moustaches and skill on horseback, has betrayed us.

Maud   Annie, Annie, be quiet while Papa goes out. It isn't Papa's fault.

Thomas   I served that King, Annie, and that will suffice me. I hope I guarded his possession well, and helped the people through a terrible time. And now that story is over and I am over with it, and content. I don't grieve.

Maud   Of course you don't. Won't we have the great days soon in Kiltegan?

Thomas   But won't Dolly miss the fashions and the shops and the to-do of the town?

Annie   (*before* **Dolly** *can answer*) I'll miss nothing. If they want to destroy everything, let them do so without us. It will be whins and waste everywhere, with bits of stones sticking up that were once Parliament, Castle and Cathedral. And people going round like scarecrows and worse. And Cuckoo Lane and Red Cow Lane and all those places just gaps with rubbish in them.

Maud   Annie, you're giving me a powerful headache.

Annie   The like of Collins and his murdering men won't hold this place together. They haven't the grace or the style for it. So you needn't mourn your shops and hats and haircuts, Dolly Dunne – they won't be there.

Thomas   Will I tell Mr Collins you said so, Annie?

Maud   You'll miss the show if you don't go now, Papa. You don't want to be running over the square to them and sweating in your finery.

Thomas   Am I shipshape?

Maud   Shipshape as a ship.

Dolly   Wait, don't let the king go! (*Hurrying out for something.*)

Thomas   Where's she off to now?

Annie   Who can say where Dolly goes.

Maud   Poor Dolly – I do feel sorry for her.

Annie   Why for Dolly? Feel sorry for yourself, woman.

Dolly (*coming back with a buttonhole*)   I got this for you last night, Papa.

Annie   On that dangerous trek back from the dance at the Rotunda . . .

Dolly (*looking at* **Annie**)   Fresh up from the country.

Annie   I hope you can wear a buttonhole today? It seems frivolous.

Thomas   Put it in for me, Dolly. A white rose! Now I'm ready for them.

Dolly (*catching sight of the heather on the table*)   Oh, but, Papa, you'd flowers already – maybe you meant to wear a bit of this?

Annie   It isn't there at all yet. Just mere hints of flowers. That heather was born in the snow.

Maud (*smelling it*)   That heather was born in the snow, right enough, Annie.

Annie (*drawn to the heather, as are* **Thomas** *and* **Dolly**)   It came up on the Wicklow train. Sometimes you find you need a hint of home.

Dolly   Born in the snow, like a lamb.

Thomas   That's from the hill beside the sloping field. I know that colour. (*Smelling, all of them smelling.*) It smells like God's breath, it does.

Maud   We won't mind going home to such riches.

Thomas   It is the very honeyed lord of a smell, so it is.

Thomas *goes out the door happily. The daughters scatter. Then the noise of a ruckus in the corridor.*

Smith (*off*)   Where are you wandering to? (*After a little.*) Where are you heading, old man?

Thomas (*off*)   What are you saying to me, constable? – Get back from me!

Smith (*off*)   Mrs O'Dea, Mrs O'Dea! Lie in there against the wall, you scarecrow, you. Mrs O'Dea! Come up, come up!

Mrs O'Dea (*off*)   Oh, I'm hurrying, I'm hurrying . . .

Mrs O'Dea *steps into the room.*

Thomas (*off*)   But I have to go and meet Collins!

Smith (*off*)   Collins is stone dead.

Thomas, *in his long johns again, propelled in by* **Smith**.

Thomas   Where are you putting me? This isn't our quarters!

Smith   Who was it left his door open? He might have gone raving up the main street of Baltinglass.

Mrs O'Dea   I don't know. It must have been his daughter.

Thomas   What have you done with my daughters? (*Pushing* **Smith**.) Get back from me, you blackguard. By Christ, assaulting a policeman. That's the Joy for you, you scoundrel.

Smith (*drawing out the pacifier*)   Right, boy, I did warn you. Now you'll get it. (*Raising the implement.*) Mrs O'Dea, fetch the

jacket off the hook in the corridor. (**Mrs O'Dea** *goes out.*)
You'll see the suit she has for you now, Thomas Dunne.

Thomas   You'll see the suit, Tomassy Tom. You'll see the
suit.

Thomas *escapes from him, leaps the bed like a youth.*

Smith   Jesus of Nazareth. (**Smith** *goes after him,* **Thomas**
ducks around to the stool, **Mrs O'Dea** *brings in the strait-jacket.*)

Thomas   Nicks, nicks.

Smith   He's claiming nicks off the three-legged stool.

Smith *strides to* **Thomas** *and strikes him with the pacifier, expertly
enough.*

Why couldn't I go with my brother flensing whales?

Thomas (*wriggling*)   You think I haven't had worse? See
this thumb? See the purple scar there? My own Da Da did
that, with a sheath knife. What do you think of that? (**Smith**
struggles to place the jacket on him.) Do you want to see my
back? I've a mark there was done with a cooper's band, and
on a Sunday too. But he loved me.

Mrs O'Dea   Lie up on your bed, Mr Dunne. (*To* **Smith**.)
He'll be worn out in a minute. I have your suit ready, Mr
Dunne, will I bring it up to you? He'll be good now, Mr
Smith.

Thomas (*lying on the bed awkwardly, bound*)   Give it to Patrick
O'Brien that excelled mightily at the bulleting. He'll eat it
piecemeal like a dog. (**Mrs O'Dea** *and* **Smith** *go out, and lock
the door.*) We're all here, the gang of us, all the heroes of my
youth, in these rooms, crying and imagining, or strung out
like poor paste pearls of people along the rows of the
graveyard. Lizzie Moran and Dorothy Cullen I saw there,
two beauties of Lathaleer, and Hannigan that killed his
mother, under a whinbush. And the five daughters of Joseph
Quinn, the five of them, much to my amazement, side by
side in five short graves. All of them lost their wits and died,
Black Jim. If I could lead those poor souls back across the

meadows and the white lanes to the hearths and niches of their youth, and fill the farms with them again, with their hopes and dreams, by God . . . I am a tired old man and I'll have terrible aches forthwith. Let him hit. What else has he, but hitting? Does he know why the calf is stupid? No. There he is in his ignorance, hitting. Let him hit. (*After a little.*) My two bonny grandsons would cure me. (*After a little.*) It's a cold wind that blows without forgiveness, as the song says.

There's a sort of darkness in the room now, with a seep of lights. **Willie** *stands in the corner, quietly, singing softly.*

My poor son . . . When I was a small child, smaller than yourself, my Ma Ma brought me home a red fire engine from Baltinglass. It was wrapped in the newspaper and hid in the hayshed for the Christmas. But I knew every nook and cranny of the hayshed, and I soon had it found, and the paper off it. And quite shortly I had invented a grand game, where I stood one foot on the engine and propelled myself across the yard. I kept falling and falling, tearing and scumming my clothes, but no matter, the game was a splendid game. And my mother she came out for something, maybe to fling the grains at the hens in that evening time, and she saw me skating on the engine and she looked at me. She looked with a terrible long face, and I looked down and there was the lovely engine all scratched and bent, and the wheel half-rubbed off it. So she took the toy quietly from under my foot, and marched over to the dunghill and shoved it in deep with her bare hands, tearing at the rubbish there and the layers of dung. So I sought out her favourite laying hen and put a yard-bucket over it, and it wasn't found for a week, by which time the Christmas was over and the poor hen's wits had gone astray from hunger and darkness and inertia. Nor did it ever lay eggs again that quickened with chicks. And that was a black time between my Ma Ma and me. (*After a little.*) You were six when your Mam died, Willie. Hardly enough time to be at war with her, the way a son might. She was very attached to you. Her son. She had a special way of talking about you, a special music in her voice. And she was proud of your singing, and knew you could make a go of it, in the halls, if you wished. I wanted to kill her when she said that. But at six you sang like a linnet, true enough. (*After a little.*) I didn't do as well as she did, with you. I was sorry you never reached six feet. I was a fool. What big loud talking fools are fathers sometimes. Why do we not love our sons simply and be done with it? She did. I would kill, or I would do a great thing, just to see you once more, in the flesh. All I got back was your uniform, with the mud only half-washed out of it. Why do they send the uniforms to the fathers and the mothers? I put it over my head and cried for a night, like an owl in a tree. I cried for a night with your uniform over my head, and no one saw me.

Mrs O'Dea *unlocks the door and comes in with the new suit, a rough black suit that she has joined with her yellow thread. She brings it to his bedside, dispelling* **Willie***.*

Mrs O'Dea   Look at the lovely thread I used in it, just like you asked. Do you think you are quiet now?

Thomas   Yes.

Mrs O'Dea *starts to untie him,* **Smith** *comes in with a bowl of food, puts it on the table.*

Mrs O'Dea (*to* **Smith**)   Help me get him into bed. He'll lie quiet. (*To* **Thomas***.*) Take off the long johns too, I'll wash them for you. (**Smith** *pulls down the top. The two wounds from the beating are revealed on* **Thomas***'s chest.*) We should put something on those weals.

Smith   He's only scratched. Let the sleep heal him. He'll spring up in the morning, gabbling as always, crazy as ever. God knows I can't deal with him now, I have a fancy dress to go to in the town.

Mrs O'Dea   Well, I can't wash a man, Mr Smith.

Smith   He doesn't need washing. He's barely marked.

Mrs O'Dea   Won't you at least wash his hands, they're all black from the floor. And I suppose his feet are as bad.

Smith   He may be St Thomas, Mrs O'Dea, but I'm not Jesus Christ, to be washing his hands and feet.

Mrs O'Dea   What is he talking about, Mr Dunne?

Smith   I have to collect my costume at six, Mrs O'Dea, off the Dublin train.

Mrs O'Dea   Tuck yourself up, Mr Dunne, and have a rest.

They go out. **Annie** *and* **Dolly** *come on in mid-conversation.*

Dolly   Where is my husband to come from, if we're to go back to Wicklow? I'm not marrying a farmer.

Annie   Oh, are you not, Dolly? Isn't it pleasant to pick and choose? What farmer would take a woman like me, and I might have had a sailor once for a husband if I'd been let. So you're not the only one with difficulties, though you always think you are. That's the way of the pretty.

Dolly   You couldn't go marrying a sailor, Annie. You never see a sailor. They're always away – sailing.

Annie   And our father humiliated by renegades. Collins!

Dolly   They didn't humiliate him, Annie, indeed, not at all. I'm sure it was all very polite. I think the truth is, Papa is delighted to be going back to Kiltegan, where he can have us all about him, slaving for him, and being his good girls, and never never marrying.

Annie   Dolly, that's poor wickedness.

Dolly   I know.

Annie   He's desolated to be going back.

Dolly   I don't believe he is. Or he'd have taken the new post in the whatever you call them. The Civic Guard.

Annie   You don't think they were offering him Chief Superintendent?

Dolly   So. Let him be a superintendent again, and stay in Dublin, where a person can buy a decent hat. There's nothing in Baltinglass but soda-bread and eggs.

Annie   There's your father struggling to put a brave face on this day, which is no doubt the death of all good things for this country, and you're worrying about hats.

Dolly   Hats are more dependable than countries.

Annie   You're a nonsensical girl, Dolly. Why don't you go away somewhere with yourself, if you don't want to go back to Wicklow?

Dolly   I might!

Annie   You will not!

Dolly   Aren't you just after telling me to?

Annie   Dolly, don't dream of going and leaving me alone in Wicklow!

Dolly   For you to be giving out to me, like I was a little girl, and telling me I mustn't think of hats?

Annie (*seriously*)   Dolly, Dolly, you wouldn't go?

Dolly   Why not?

Annie (*almost shaking her.*)   Dolly, I'm serious, say you wouldn't. (*After a little.*) Say you wouldn't.

Dolly   All right, all right, I wouldn't! I wouldn't. I wouldn't, Annie, dear.

Annie *nods at her fiercely. They go off.*

Thomas (*from the bed*)   I could scarce get over the sight of him. He was a black-haired handsome man, but with the big face and body of a boxer. He would have made a tremendous policeman in other days. He looked to me like Jack Dempsey, one of those prize-fighting men we admired. I would have been proud to have him as my son. When he walked he was sort of dancing, light on his pins, like a good bulleter. Like Patrick O'Brien himself. He looked like he might give Patrick O'Brien a good challenge for his money on some evening road somewhere, hoisting that ball of granite. He had glamour about him, like a man that goes about with the fit-ups, or one of those picture stars that came on the big ship from New York, to visit us, and there'd be crowds in the streets like for royalty, and it would be a fierce job to keep them held back. Big American men and women, twice the size of any Irish person. And some of them Irish too, but fed those many years on beef and wild turkeys. He was like that, Mr Collins. I felt rough near him, that cold morning, rough, secretly. There never was enough gold in that uniform, never. I thought too as I looked at him of my father, as if Collins could have been my son and could have been my father. I had risen as high as a Catholic could go, and there wasn't enough braid, in the upshot. I remembered my father's anger when I failed at my schooling, and how he said he'd put me into the police, with the other fools of Ireland. I knew that by then most of the men in my division were for Collins, that they would have followed him wherever he wished, if he had called them. And for an instant, as the Castle was signed over to him, I felt a shadow of that loyalty pass across my heart. But I closed my heart instantly against it. We were to have peace. On behalf of the Crown the chief secretary wished him well. And indeed it was peaceful, that moment. The savagery and ruin that soon followed broke my heart again and again and again. My streets and squares became places for murder and fire. All that spring and summer, as now and then some brave boy spat at me in the streets, I could not hold back the tide of ruin. It was a personal matter. We had restored order in the days of Larkin. One morning I met a man in St Stephen's Green. He was looking at a youngster thrown half-in under a bush. No more than eighteen. The man himself was one of that army of ordinary, middle-class Irishmen with firm views and moustaches. He was apoplectic. We looked at each other. The birds were singing pleasantly, the early sun was up. 'My grandsons,' he said, 'will be feral in this garden – mark my words.'

Dolly, **Maud** and **Annie** *come on and move* **Thomas**'s *table out a little and start to half-set it. There's a knock, and* **Matt** *appears.*

Annie   Who are you? What do you want?

Dolly   Who is that, Annie?

Annie   What do you want here?

Matt   My name's Matthew Kirwin, ma'am. I was asked to supper by Maud Dunne.

Annie   By Maud Dunne?

Maud (*coming over*)   Oh, hello, Mr Kirwin. How kind of you to come.

Annie   How kind of him to come?

Maud   Come in, Mr Kirwin, and meet my sisters. This is Dolly.

Dolly   How do you do?

Maud   And this is Annie.

Annie   Yes, this is Annie. And who is this, Maud?

Maud   My friend, Annie, Mr Matthew Kirwin.

Annie   Since when do you have friends, Maud, coming to supper?

Maud   I suppose I can have friends just as soon as Dolly? I suppose I can.

Annie   And have you known Mr Kirwin long, Maud?

Maud   We have an acquaintance. Mr Kirwin was painting in Stephen's Green last Saturday, and I happened to look over his shoulder at what he was doing, and as a matter of fact he was quite cross with me, weren't you, Mr Kirwin, for doing so, and we fell to talking then, and I explained my interest in the old masters . . .

Annie   Your interest in the old masters?

Maud   Yes, Annie. And we both agreed that the newer type of painters were all mad, and I invited him to supper.

Annie (*almost pushing him back*)   I'm sorry, Mr Kirwin, but you'll have to go.

Maud   Annie Dunne!

Annie   I don't know how you got past the gates, but there are to be no strangers coming in here. (*Pushing him elegantly.*)

Matt   If it isn't convenient . . .

Annie   It isn't even desirable, Mr Kirwin.

Maud   Annie, lay your hands off that man, he is my artist that I found in Stephen's Green.

Annie   And do you go out into the street, these times, Maud, and shake hands with everyone you see, and ask them to supper, if they are not doing anything better that night?

Maud   I do not, Annie Dunne.

Annie   What do you know about a man like this, with the leisure to be painting in daylight . . .

Matt   It was my day off, Miss Dunne . . .

Annie   And with a foreign accent . . .

Matt   I'm from Cork city . . .

Annie   And who may be the greatest rogue or the greatest saint that ever came out of – Cork city . . .

Maud   You are not my mother, Annie, in fact I am older and wiser than you . . .

Dolly   Let him stay till Papa comes, Annie, and if Papa says he is all right, we can have him to supper. It would be lovely to have friends to supper again. Let's, Annie.

Annie   And if he is an assassin?

Dolly   He's just a young man like any other young man.

Annie So are assassins. No, it cannot be. (*Pushing him more vigorously.*) Out with you, Mr Kirwin.

Maud Leave him be, oh, Annie, leave him be! (*She seems faint now, her legs buckling under her.*) Leave my artist be . . .

Dolly *tries to hold her up.*

Dolly Help me, please.

Matt *holds her too.*

Annie Let go of her, let go of her!

Maud *falls to the ground.*

Dolly Oh, Annie, look what you've done now. Now we're the assassins, and Maud is killed.

The banging of a door below.

Annie That's Papa. Papa always bangs the lower door for us, Mr Kirwin, because he has a house of girls. Now you'll get your supper!

Matt I assure you, Miss Dunne . . .

Thomas *comes from the bed and stops by them. He doesn't speak.* **Maud** *opens her eyes, looks at him, gets up.* **Dolly** *goes and kisses her father.*

Dolly What is it, Papa? You look so pale.

Maud Do you have a chill, Papa?

Matt (*to* **Annie**) I'll go, I'll go . . .

Annie (*not hearing him*) Are you all right, Papa?

Thomas (*after a little*) The city is full of death. (*After a little, crying.*) The city is full of death.

Annie (*hissing, to* **Maud**) Look at the state Papa is in – it's no night for a visitor.

Thomas How do you do, how do you do.

Maud (*to* **Matt**) By the pillar, Saturday noon.

Matt *nods and goes.*

Thomas   Do I smell a stew, a real stew? Is that the aroma of lamb, bless me?

Annie   It is, Papa.

Thomas   Where did you get lamb, Annie?

Annie   The Dunnes of Feddin sent it up. It's Wicklow lamb.

Thomas   Wicklow. It is – Elysium. It is paradise . . . We'll be happy there, girls . . .

Annie   We will, Papa. We'll fetch the supper, Papa.

But they go out taking the things from the table with them. The door unlocks behind **Thomas**, *and* **Smith** *enters with a basin and a bottle of ointment. He is dressed like a cowboy complete with six-shooters.* **Thomas** *stares at him.*

Thomas   Black Jim!

Smith   Ah, never let it be said I left you alone with those cuts. Come here and sit, if you will. (**Thomas** *obediently goes to the stool.* **Smith** *puts down the bowl and begins to tend to* **Thomas**.) What's got into me? There's a lovely party going on in the town.

Thomas   I could be a man war-wounded.

Smith   You could. Or the outcome of a punch-up in a western saloon.

Thomas (*laughing*)   You think so?

Smith (*posing with the ointment*)   Do I not remind you of anyone in this get-up?

Thomas (*trying*)   No.

Smith   Maybe you never fancied the pictures, did you?

Thomas   I went the odd time to the magic lanthorn show.

Smith   You couldn't guess then who I am, besides being Mr Smith, I mean?

Thomas   Black Jim?

Smith   Gary Cooper, Gary Cooper. Ah, you're no use.

Thomas   Gary Cooper? Is that the Coopers of Rathdangan?

Smith (*putting on the ointment*)   *Lilac Time.* Did you never catch that? You haven't lived. Of course, it wasn't a cowboy as such. *Redemption* was a hell of a good cowboy.

Thomas   No man is beyond redemption, my Ma Ma said, when he let the dog live.

Smith   Who, Thomas? If men were beyond redemption, Thomas, what would we do in Ireland for Presidents?

Thomas   That's a fair question. (*Laughing.*)

Smith (*doing a cowboy*)   You dirty dog, you dirty dog. (*After a little.*) Did you go to the war, Thomas?

Thomas   Me? No – I was too old. My son was with the Dublin Rifles.

Smith   Oh, I think I knew that. He was the boy that was killed.

Thomas   He was that boy.

Smith   I had a first cousin in it. A lot of men went out.

Thomas   Did he come home?

Smith   Not at all. They sent the uniform.

Thomas   That's right, they do. I've only a letter from him, that's all I have in the world of him.

Smith   Written from the battlefield?

Thomas   Oh, aye, from the trenches themselves.

Smith   I'd be very interested to see that letter.

Thomas   Would you, Mr Smith? Of course. I have it somewhere, stuck in Annie's book. Will I get it?

Smith   Do, get it, man, and we'll have a read of it. Why not?

Thomas (*fetching the letter*)   Do you not want to get to your fancy dress?

Smith   The party can wait. (*Taking the old letter.*) It looks old enough.

Thomas   Well, it's coming up to twenty year ago now.

Smith (*opening it carefully*)   It's an historical document.

Thomas (*laughing*)   Oh, aye. Historical.

Smith (*reading*)   He has a good hand at the writing, anyhow. (*Reading.*)

Thomas (*nudging his knee*)   Would you not . . .

Smith   Read it aloud? You want me to?

Thomas   I do. I would greatly like that.

Smith   Fair enough. Okay. (*Settling himself to read it, clearing his voice, a little self-conscious.*) Of course, I don't read aloud much, so . . . (**Thomas** *smiles*.) Right. – My dearest Papa, Here I am writing to you in the midst of all these troubles. We are three weeks now in the one spot and we all feel we are dug in here for an eternity. The shells going over have become familiar to us, and my friend the first lieutenant from Leitrim, Barney Miles, has given our regular rats names. Our first idea was to thump them with spades because they eat the corpses up on the field but surely there has been enough death. We have not got it as bad as some companies, because our position is raised, and we get drainage, but all the same we know what real mud is by now. We have had some miracles, in that last week deep in the night one of our men was thrown back over the rampart wounded, by what hands we do not know. Another man was sent out with a dispatch and on his way back found a big sow thrashing in the mud. He would have taken her on with him for chops except she was twice his weight and not keen. It made us remember that all hereabout was once farms, houses and farms and grass and stock, and surely the farmer in you would weep, Papa, to see the changes. I hope you don't mind my letter going on. It gives me great comfort to write to my father. You will probably think I am raving a bit, and ranting, but nevertheless, since I am so far distant, I tell myself you will be interested to get news of me here. I wish I could tell you that I am a hero, but truth to tell, there are few opportunities for valour, in the way we all imagined when we set out. I have not seen the enemy. Sometimes in the dark and still of the night-times I see lights over where their position is, and on the stillest evenings you can just hear their voices. Sometimes they sing! Sometimes we sing, low and quiet, we have quite a repertoire now of risky songs, that you wouldn't approve at all. But it is a grand thing that we can still use our voices, and when I sing I think of home, and my sisters, and my father, and hope and know that my mother is watching over me here. God keep you all safe, because we have been told of the ruckus at home, and some of the country men are as much upset by that as they would be by their present emergency. I know you are in the front line there, Papa, so keep yourself safe for my return, when Maud will cook the fatted calf! The plain truth is, Papa, this is a strange war and a strange time, and my whole wish is to be home with you all in Dublin, and to abide by your wishes, whatever they be. I wish to be a more dutiful son because, Papa, in the mire of this wasteland, you stand before my eyes as the finest man I know, and in my dreams you comfort me, and keep my spirits lifted. Your son, Willie.

Thomas (*after a little, while* **Smith** *folds the letter and gives it back to him*)   In my dreams you comfort me . . .

Smith   That's a beautiful letter, Mr Dunne. A memento. A keepsake.

Thomas *nods his head, thinking.*

(*Getting up to go.*) Good man, good man. (*Goes, locks the door.*)

Thomas *puts away his letter and climbs into bed. After a little* **Dolly** *enters and goes to his bedside, with a big ticket in her hand.* **Thomas** *looks at her, takes the ticket, reads it, looks at her.*

Dolly You aren't angry, Papa? It took all my courage to buy it, every ounce I had, you can't imagine. (*After a little.*) You are wondering how I could afford it? It was quite expensive, but it's only steerage. I had to sell Mam's bracelet that I was given, the ruby one you gave me, and I've to work for an agency the first two years, as a domestic, in Cleveland, Ohio.

Thomas (*after a little*) Is it because she died on us? She was mortally sorry to die. She died as the need for candlelight failed. She would have adored you, even as she gave her life for you.

Dolly Papa, don't be angry with me, please, I could not bear it, it took all my courage.

Thomas Why would you go, Dolly, that is loved by us all, and young men going crazy over you here, and queuing up to marry you?

Dolly They're not, Papa. I want to be liked and loved, but people are cold towards me, Papa.

Thomas Why would they be, Dolly?

Dolly Because – because of you, Papa, I suppose.

Thomas It will pass, Dolly. In Wicklow we will be among our own people.

Dolly I don't want to be like the Dunnes of Feddin, three wild women with unkept hair and slits on the backs of their hands from ploughing. You're old, Papa, it's not the same for you.

Thomas (*smiling, giving back the ticket*) Yes, I am old.

Dolly I didn't mean to say that, Papa. I knew you would be angry with me, I prayed you wouldn't be.

Thomas Come here to me. (*He embraces her.*) How could I be angry with you? It's a poor look-out if I am angry with my own baby because she is afraid.

Dolly I didn't want to hurt you, Papa.

Thomas Papa is strong enough for all these things.

Dolly   You'll take care, Papa, and write to me, about all the goings-on in Kiltegan?

Thomas   I will of course. (*The lock turns in the door,* **Dolly** *breaks from him, goes.*) I will of course!

Mrs O'Dea *pops in and places a pair of black shoes by his bed.*

Mrs O'Dea   I'm just putting these here for you. I found you shoes at last, to go with the beautiful suit. I didn't mean to disturb you. You're the neatest sleeper I ever did meet, Mr Dunne. Never a ruffle in the sheets, just a long warm nest where your body lies.

Thomas   That's about the height of it.

Mrs O'Dea   Oh, you're a man for a bit of philosophy, I know.

Thomas   Whose shoes were they, Mrs O'Dea?

Mrs O'Dea   Let's see now. They were Patrick O'Brien's, Mr Dunne.

Thomas (*after a moment*)   You must take them for another man. I'd never fill them.

Mrs O'Dea   But what if your grandsons come to see you and you've nothing to put on your feet?

Thomas   There's no chance of that now.

Mrs O'Dea (*taking up the bowl of food*)   It's stone cold and you ate nothing. (*Going.*) Didn't I make you a beautiful suit?

She goes, locks the door. **Annie** *comes on with one of his big socks to darn and sits on the stool and works on the darning.* **Thomas** *dons* **Mrs O'Dea**'s *suit.*

Annie   Three days now, Papa.

Thomas   Three days, Annie. And we'll be set up in the old house again. We'll get that dairy going again first thing, a good scrub-down with the carbolic.

Annie   Yes.

Thomas   And I'll have our milking cow fetched over from Feddin, and the Dunnes of Feddin can hire someone else's fields, because we'll need them presently.

Annie   We will.

Thomas   And we'll be dog tired every night from the wealth of work, and be proud. And we have eight Rhode Island Reds and a crowing cock, that they are keeping for me in Lathaleer. And they're looking out for a pony, they say they know a fair-minded tinker will sell us something apt, and two hours at the most with a pot of polish will have those high lamps on the old trap gleaming. And we will cut a fine figure, you and I, Annie, Thomas Dunne and his daughter, throughout Kiltegan, Feddin and Kelsha.

Annie   We'll enjoy ourselves.

Thomas   And I'll lime the whole place. The house will be blinding white. We'll have red geraniums on the sills like the very dark conscience of summer or we're not Christians at all.

Annie   And Maud to visit, and we'll be peering at her, you know? (*Winking.*)

Thomas   And letters from Dolly, in the meantime, till she wishes to come home.

A knocking. The **Recruit**, *now a constable, comes on.* **Annie** *goes to him. The* **Constable** *whispers in her ear.* **Annie** *comes back to* **Thomas**.

Annie   It's one of the constables, Papa. He wants a word with you privately.

Thomas *goes over to him. The* **Constable** *whispers to him.*
Thomas *at length pats the man briefly on the arm. The* **Constable** *goes.* **Thomas** *returns slowly to* **Annie**.

What, Papa?

Thomas   They have killed Collins in Cork.

Annie (*after a little*)   We'll be doubly glad to be going home now, and free of it all, Papa.

Thomas *can say nothing*.

Doubly glad.

A country music, and the wide ash-glow of a fire in the grate.

Thomas (*to himself*)   She died as many persons do, at the death of candlelight, as the birds begin to sing. She was a child again at the end, as if she was back again years ago in Lathaleer, and talking to her father, Cullen the coppicer. I stood by her bed, holding Dolly in my arms like a three-pound bag of loose corn, and Cissy spoke to me as if I were her own father. But our account was clear. (*Calling.*) Annie! When I went out that day to stop Larkin in Sackville Street, all the world of my youth, the world of Ireland that I knew, was still in place, loyal, united and true. I had three lovely daughters, and a little son as glad as a rose. And I had risen as high as Catholic could in the Dublin Metropolitan Police. And we were drawn up, ready to dispell them. (*Sits in near fire.*) Annie!

Annie   Yes, Papa?

Thomas   Bring my sword, would you?

Annie   No, Papa, I'm not bringing your sword.

Thomas   There's fellas roaming the countryside seeking out the maiming of this man and the death of that man, old scores must be settled, they're whispering and conspiring in the dark.

Annie   There's nothing and no one out there, Papa.

Thomas   But there is. I can smell them. Dark boys in black suits bought off the back of carts in county fairs, with old guns that might as soon blow off their own fingers when they fire. They won't get us. You must bring the sword.

Annie   There's nothing but your own fears. Go in to your bed and pull the blankets over your face and get a sleep, Papa.

Thomas   And lose my last daughter to ruffians and murderers?

Annie   You have the respect of the district, Papa.

Thomas   And what about that filthy mass of men that came up the yard last week and rattled our latch, and shouted in at me, while you were away at the well?

Annie   It was only a crowd of tinkers, Papa, that thought you were a woman alone, and wanted to frighten you. They took two churns from the shed and a length of rope because you wouldn't go out to them.

Thomas   I didn't dare breathe, I didn't dare breathe. I held fast to the fire.

Annie   Papa, you know country life better than me, but you are not suited to it, I think.

A soughing in the maples outside.

Thomas   There's them breathing now. Fetch the sword!

The soughing. **Thomas** *bolts from the stool and gets the sword, comes back and stands in the middle of the room holding it high.*

Come in now to us, and see what you'll get!

Annie   Papa, Papa, please. (*She tries to hold him and take the sword.*) If you'll be quiet, I'll make us another pot of tea and then we can go to our rest.

Thomas (*breaking from her*)   I must strike, I must strike. (*He goes about hitting at whatever he can, table and stool and such.*) Look at them running about like rats! Annie, there's rats come in, down the chimney! (*Striking the floor.*) Look at them, they're too quick for me!

Annie   There's no rats in my house! (*She covers her face with her hands.*) It's a clean house.

Thomas (*raving*)   What a to-do and a turmoil it is, with all their heroes lying in state about the city! They're bringing him up tonight to lie in state in the Pro-cathedral! Collins!

We'll be doubly glad to be going home, now, she said!
Because of you, Papa, I suppose, says Dolly. Says Dolly, says
Dolly, says Dolly, says Dolly . . .

Annie   Papa! Stop it!

*He does. He stands still where he is, the sword loose in his grip. He
breathes heavily. He sinks to his knees, offers* **Annie** *the sword.*

Thomas   Please, child . . .

Annie   What now?

Thomas   I am quiet now, Annie. I ask you a simple favour.

Annie   What favour, Papa?

Thomas   Take the sword, Annie, and raise it up like a
slash-hook, and bring it down on top of me like I was
brambles, with all your might.

Annie *looks at him. She goes to him and pulls the sword roughly
from him. Maybe she considers using it for a moment. She goes, taking
the sword with her.* **Thomas** *stares after her. He closes his eyes and
cries like a child. The fire fades away, and the colder light of his room
in the Baltinglass home returns.* **Willie** *comes, his uniform flecked
with gold.*

Thomas (*head down*)   Da Da, Ma Ma, Ba Ba . . . (*After a
little, seeing his son.*)   Oh, Willie . . . (*Humorously.*) The great
appear great because we are on our knees. Let us rise.

Willie *holds out a hand to help him get up.* **Thomas** *is surprised to
find it solid enough when he takes it.*

Oh, Willie . . .

Willie *brings him over to the bed and helps him get in.*

It's all topsy-turvy, Willie. (*After a little.*) Sure, Willie, I
think the last order I gave to the men was to be sure and
salute Mr Collins's coffin as it went by . . . (*After a little.*)
One time, Willie, and it was Christmastime too, and I was a
young fellow in Kiltegan, our dog Shep went missing for
some days, as dogs in winter will. I was maybe ten or eleven,

and I loved that Shep, and feared he was gone forever. We had got him as a young dog that had been beaten somewhere, and broken, till he reached our haven, and uncoiled, and learned to bark like a baby learns to laugh, and he shone at his work.

Willie *gets up on the bed beside his father.*

One morning early after a fall of snow I went out to break the ice on the rain-barrel to plash my face, and I saw his tracks in the snow going up the sloping field, high to the fringes of the wood, and I was greatly afeared, because there were drops of blood now and then as he went, little smears of it on the cleanly snow. So I followed him up, sinking here and there in the drifts, well used to it, well used to it, and on a piece of field we called the upper garden, because it was flat there and you could see across to Baltinglass and some said even to Shillelagh and the dark woods of Coollattin, I found our dog there with the carcass of a ewe well-eaten, only the hindquarters remaining. I saw my father's blue sign on the wool and knew the worst. For a dog that would kill a sheep would die himself. So in my innocence I went down to my father and told him and he instructed me, as was right and proper, to go back up with a rope and lead Shep down so the killing could take place. The loss of a ewe was a disaster, a disaster, there'd be pounds of money gone into her. But I loved the dog so sorely, I hesitated when I had the rope tied about him, and at length led him off further up the hill, across the little stand of scrubby pines, and on into the low woods dark with snow and moss. And we went through by a snaking path I knew, till we got to the other side, where there was a simple man living, that made his living from the rabbits, and maybe had need of a watchful dog. But he wouldn't take a dog that had killed, though he was a tender man enough, and it behoved me to retrace my steps back into the woods, now moving along but slowly, and the dog sort of dragging behind, as if he knew well his misdeed and his fate. And I stopped in the centre of the trees, and do you know my young legs would not go forward, they would not proceed, try as I might, and there I was all that afternoon and night with the dog and the hazels. How is it that the drear of winter didn't eat my bones and murder me for my foolishness? Love of the dog kept me standing there, as only a child can stand, without moving, thinking, the poor dog whimpering with the cold. About five o'clock I went on, because I heard calling over the hill, here and there, and I could see black figures with lights moving and calling, calling out to me and the dog to come home. We came down the sloping field with the neighbours about us, them not saying a word, maybe marvelling at me, thinking I had been dead, and the torches and lamps making everything crazy with light, the old crab apple enlarging to the size of the field, its branches wild like arms. Down at last into the yard we came, the dog skulking on the rope just the same as the day he had arrived to us, and my father came out from the house in his big clothes. All brown with clothes and hair. It was as if I had never seen him before, never looked at him in his entirety, from head to toe. And I knew then that the dog and me were for slaughter. My feet carried me on to where he stood, immortal you would say in the door. And he put his right hand on the back of my head, and pulled me to him so that my cheek rested against the buckle of his belt. And he raised his own face to the brightening sky and praised someone, in a crushed voice, God maybe, for my safety, and stroked my hair. And the dog's crime was never spoken of, but that he lived till he died. And I would call that the mercy of fathers, when the love that lies in them deeply like the glittering face of a well is betrayed by an emergency, and the child sees at last that he is loved, loved and needed and not to be lived without, and greatly.

He sleeps. **Willie** *lies in close to him. Sleeps. Music. Dark.*

White Woman Street

For Jim

Characters

Trooper O'Hara, *in his fifties, left Sligo in his youth, a red-headed man, narrow-faced, dark*
Blakely, *from Lincolnshire originally, now in his fifties, dark-haired, round-faced, lined, reddened*
Mo Mason, *from an Amish community in Ohio, in his seventies, a full man, still has his hair, not tall*
Nathaniel Yeshov, *from Brooklyn, Russian father, Chinese mother, the appearance of an eastern Russian, small, in his thirties*
James Miranda, *from Tennessee, black, about thirty or younger, the nearest to handsome of any of them, bright*
Clarke, *native American, from Virginia, in his seventies*

The play is set in Ohio, and in the small town of White Woman Street, in 1916.

White Woman Street was first performed at the Bush Theatre, London, on 23 April 1992, with the following cast:

Trooper	Jim Norton
Blakely	George Irving
Mo	Roy Hanlon
Nathaniel	David Yip
James	Patrick Miller
Clarke	Kevork Malikyan

Director Caroline Fitzgerald
Designer Kendra Ullyart
Lighting Tina MacHugh
Music Shaun Davey

Act One

Deep shadow downstage, five rough bed-sites ranged about a wood fire, burned down to a redness. A shaky set-up across the fire, a coffee can at the side, cups knocked together. Four of the men are asleep in their blankets, their possessions by them, leathers, guns, hats. The other blanket, red-dyed, is pulled aside, empty. Five 'horses' are tethered upstage. A local music, quietly. First light. Gold and red edges freshen the shadows near the 'horses', where **Trooper** *stands with his rifle. The light colours* **Trooper**, *dressed in old army clothes and other items. He's watching the sun rising in a scoop of land beyond the trees.*

Trooper (*alone to himself*) You could stand on the back step of an April morning and watch the men go up with lights to fire the gorse. That was how gorse could be managed. You could stand there watching as a boy and hear the hot sound start in the distance there and the deep red fires begin to mark the hills, scraps of it, as if hares were sitting up in the gorse, all aflame from the sun rising behind their fur. You could hear the cock crowing in the deep valley, and you could hear the farmer there stirring up his horse to lead it out into the yard to be hitched to the yard-arm of the butter churn. Then round and round that horse would walk till the wife tapped on the window of the dairy when the butter came at last, and the farmer wouldn't hear but the horse always did, and stopped. And up behind him would come the following yard-arm and knock him in the hocks, and the farmer cursing then. And when that farmer was ploughing in the autumn he would bring his horse to his neighbour's horse for the yoke. That selfsame gorse they cut then with the stubbing-axe and fed the crushed root to the horse for to make him strong to plough. And if the neighbour's horse hadn't had the whins, why it would smell the whins off the breath of the farmer's horse, and wouldn't work in the trace. For you had to give them both the whins. And then in the winter we were back in Sligo town for my father's business and my schooling, and we left the cock to crow in the growing cold till Easter following, when the gorse would be lit again. And by evening of that spring day, when the butter of the world came, and the yard-arm of the world followed round and knocked my legs, the half of the hills would be burning, and you could see something, maybe the shape of America all deep yellow with high flames and a fume of smoke.

The long lights creeping into the camp, ropes of sunlight approaching the sleeping men.

They were things I left when I myself began to fume with youth and had the silver for a ticket to Cork, and for the ship of sails to New York. And I traded my gorse and my father and my Sligo for an army horse whose saddle became my home, and I was out among the Indian wars. And when too weary to do that work I looked about me but was good for nothing. So one day and the darkest of my life I rode into a young town of those days called White Woman Street, where the canal workers and the troopers went to visit the famous whore, the only white woman for five hundred miles. And I was keen to see her and my heart was sore and I was needing a hint of home. And in I went to her.

A wind blows in further light.

So thirty years ago not far from here I saw the worst sight of all my days and I hit the roads of America as a simple outlaw and followed that trade. And I was a different man from that time on, and my heart was a kind of hidden hill where at the last hour of the night men got up and climbed it with fires and fired the rampant gorse. So now with memories of home I aim to head for home again and rest a local man in Sligo. But I can't go till peace is made, till I stand again in White Woman Street, and beg a certain ghost for her good word. In this filthied land of thinning trees, to send Trooper home. At Easter here, in Ohio.

The wind heaps in shadow across **Trooper**. *A blade of gold sunlight touches* **Mo**'s *face. He rubs at it, grunts, locates his old hat without looking, sets it across his eyes.* **Blakely** *wakes abruptly, fumbles for his rifle, looks about, hits the side of his head to get it working.*

Blakely   How's that now, Mo? – You waked, Mo? – I could feel fellas creeping up.

Mo (*from under his hat*)   Who, brother?

Blakely   Blackfoot, Crowfoot, some class of foot – Redmen.

Mo (*peering out*)   Not none of them running around Ohio these times. Redmen drinking and praying in Ohio now. You'd fear more from bears. Preachers couldn't convince *them* to leave off their wild habits.

Blakely   Don't I like to drink and pray myself – when I can. Where does Trooper be?

Nathaniel *throws off his blanket.*

Nathaniel (*stretching*)   Sorry to leave paradise. Dreamed I was there. Loose women – lovely, lovely loose women all about me. Silk drawers, gents.

Mo   I'n't he there in his nest?

Blakely   No, sir. My guess he be up in a tree stealing honey, or a-running after some varmint for his breakfast. Maybe your bears sneaked up and dragged him away, Mo.

Mo   No, he be crushing daisies and such, most like, finding a quiet spot for himself.

Trooper *comes downstage, fixing the braces on his old trousers.*

Blakely   Morning, Trooper. Any luck?

Trooper   Why do I lick that rock sugar when I know what it does? (*He sits himself down near* **Mo**.)

Mo   That human nature.

Blakely (*seeing* **James** *still asleep*)   Someone wake that poor sleeping man. Nathaniel, wake that bosom pal of yours.

Trooper   When you wake him, we can be talking. I got something fixed now.

Mo   He maybe weary still, Blakely.

Blakely   Weary – but he know where the coffee-grinds is.

Mo   Wake him up, Nathaniel. (*To* **Trooper**.) If you feeling poorly, brother, I can be boiling hogweed for that.

Trooper (*shaking his head*)   No . . .

Nathaniel (*shaking* **James**)   Rising up now, Jim, why don't you? (*Shakes some more.*)

Blakely   That man thinks he got the right to freeze up every morning of his life now. We got to wake a man from the living dead to get a cup of coffee.

Nathaniel *works at* **James**.

Trooper   He got a government bullet in his back somewhere.

Blakely   West Virginia. But that three year ago now. His black nose twitched.

Mo   Log in a little river can work the same mischief.

James's *eyes open.*

Blakely   Hallelujah. (*Waving a hand.*) You there, Jim? Where the coffee?

James (*to* **Blakely**)   Good morning, Mr Whisky.

Blakely   That a nice thing to call me, Jim, and me sworn off liquor. I'm going to fill me now all right, with that coffee. Where is that coffee?

James *rises stiffly and starts to ready the coffee.*

Mo   That thoughtful God made us a sweet morning.

Trooper   Southern Ohio weather, can't best it. I watched the mist lift off the valley. Where it goes no creature knows. The woods get gold when the old sun starts his rising. This be bare country, but a fella can gaze happy at dawn.

Mo   Come May, you seeing that shining dogwood, blossom of home – Ohio i'n't so bare then. Right honest weather for

an old man, and from Ohio in his early days at that.
Familiar to me, this springing weather.

Blakely   Mo, Mo, you the chicken of spring.

Trooper   Well, boys, you may be wondering these last days
why I bringing you through these empty lands. Why we
setting our horses over fields without a harvest sown. Why
we wandering through these thin woods.

Nathaniel   Just most of the world strange to us, Trooper.
None of this more special.

Mo   You fixing something, Trooper?

Trooper   I fixing something. I know a gold train . . .

Nathaniel   You know a gold train?

Trooper   I know one, passes through a town two days from
here.

Nathaniel (*to* **James**)   A gold train.

Mo   You been at this town, Trooper?

Trooper   I been. Maybe thirty years ago.

Nathaniel   That so?

Mo   Mightn't be running there these times. You know if it
is?

Trooper   No. But I believe it does. I hoping it does. Army
train, and army train tends to run regular enough through
the years.

Blakely   Worth a look-see.

Trooper   I got to look-see, anyways.

Mo   I can hope too in this train of hope, Trooper.

Trooper   You all want to go and check?

Blakely   Sure. (*Looking around at the others.*)

Trooper   Jim?

James   Gold train? I don't mind being a rich man. You got James Miranda.

Trooper   All right then. Two days.

The light fuller now. **James** *hands round the cups. The men nod to him in turn, glad to get it. A small ritual.* **Blakely** *stirs himself.*

Blakely   Black hot coffee suits this man. What you say to another month, and summer?

Mo   Optimistic, like the fella said.

Trooper   Some dark grievous winter anyhow.

Blakely   A dark winter for poor robbermen without no homes. Blackest rain all through. Never saw such dribbling and weeping of the skies. Need a gold train . . .

Mo   God listening, Blakely. Luck in silence.

Blakely   I know. Just rambling.

James (*sitting down with his cup*)   Water in winter, sweat in summer, two useless thing that everyone got.

Blakely   That some of your southern lore, Jim?

Trooper   Whaling man I knew once, in Nantucket, wore the best skins I ever saw. There weren't any rain of earth could drench him, he were so wrapped in those skins. He had a hat just as steep as a mountain, a black thing. Gold man he was, in his yellow skins, in the prow of a storming ship. Could take any weight of sea on his head and just shake the sea off. A gold man.

Blakely (*as if putting up an umbrella over himself, and pursing his lips*)   Make rain-umbrellas from whale-ribs, they do. Maybe be raining in the night – see any whale spouts out on these green seas lately? There, there she breaches!

Nathaniel (*rising up laughing*)   Making corsets too out of them ribs. See any corsets?

Laughter.

(*Sinking down again.*)   See the same scarcity, women and whales, out here.

Trooper (*a little excited*)   You'll see women now in White Woman Street. You'll see plenty good women. I know. You'll see those Indian women waiting for you, in those high-stockinged dresses. That's what you'll see there.

Mo *looking at* **Trooper**, **Blakely** *at* **Mo**.

Blakely (*after a little*)   Hate to rob a nice town like that.

Trooper   Not robbing it. That train i'n't the possession of that town. That a through-going train, Blakely. We can be moral men there in that town, believe me.

James (*poking about in a leather sack*)   Best buy some stores afore we chance the train. Going to be stewing up hickory in the mornings otherwise.

Blakely   You want to go and store-shop elegantwise before you take all that glistening gold off of that good through-going train?

James   You care for that Jim's coffee, don't you? We got three spoons left of it to sprinkle now.

Blakely   Sure, sure, Jim.

James   That's it.

Trooper   Don't be saying again we be robbing that town, you hear, Blakely?

Blakely (*attacked from another direction*)   Sure, sure, Trooper.

Nathaniel   You try them nice Indian girls, Trooper?

Blakely (*generally*)   Anyone else care to grizzle me?

Trooper   I didn't have no money then – not for wild women. That's thirty years gone by and I'm as short now for them grinning eagles.

Blakely (*making up*)   I thinking too, you don't got no money now, Trooper.

Trooper   That don't matter to me.

Nathaniel   We got enough for girls, Blakely?

Blakely   I'n't you a robberman, Nathaniel?

Nathaniel   I should think so.

Mo   They have a bath-house in White Woman Street there, Trooper?

Trooper   Not those thirty years ago. Maybe it's a big, upjumped, civilised place now.

Mo   Could steep for a Monday. I believe, I believe I got the dirt of last fall under the dirt of winter just gone by, and now here's the dirt of this spring weather, dust and birdshit and such devilment.

Blakely   That's all as good as a raincoat, Mo.

Mo   Rain touches this, just lightly, Mo Mason turns into a quagmire. That the word, i'n't it, Trooper? You the scholar.

Trooper   Why, Mo, certainly is.

Mo   A quagmire.

Nathaniel   You doubtless is a funny old man, Mo.

Mo   I doubtless am.

Blakely   Doubtless!

He directs the grit of his coffee into the fire and the others expertly follow suit. **Trooper** *drifts left alone, the others take up their gear and ready the horses. They move slowly, fixing their guns, their hats.* **Blakely** *dons his long travelling coat.* **Trooper** *seems apart, in another light, of new green shadows. A local music.*

Trooper   Berry-gathering. One day she comes in with red gloves, as she might say, the next blue. Maybe purple, maybe the strange stain of the elderberry. All them things would turn up later in bottles – local wine. I don't know if she lives. People in Sligo who knew her said she could make a good wine out of haws – a thing rarely done. Or better, yewberries, the killer of cows. Maybe the ma done that. Maybe her arms smelled so good because she was forever scrubbing them – scrubbing off the juices – in that white tin basin with burning soap. Sometimes her arms were just rainbows. She smelled of the fires of soap. A young woman making wine for her husband's friends. Making all them wines. And scrubbing. I don't know if she lives.

The light spreading about the others. **Trooper** *fixing his stuff.*

Blakely   What time of the clock is it, Trooper? For a man who i'n't hurrying.

Trooper (*looking at his fob-watch*)   What time of the blessed clock? 'Tis now ten good minutes past the hour.

Blakely   Which hour is that, Trooper?

Trooper (*pocketing his watch, mounting*)   The seventh hour, Blakely.

Time shifting, a local music, the wild meadowlight around them, walking slowly, the blow of birds, the dart of things, bright flies, beams, sparkling. The men settled, easy, in the little heave of the horses.

Blakely   Man such as me likes to travel through such bleak districts, through these old ash woods and broken pine. Gladdens a Lincolnshire boy. What day now we likely to gain White Woman Street, Trooper?

Trooper (*to himself*)   To beg a certain ghost . . .

Blakely *rests back in his 'saddle'.*

Blakely   Huh?

Trooper *stirs himself.*

Trooper   One more night with the owls. (**Blakely** *cheered, responding.*) And tomorrow, gents, we see that town below us. Little place bunched in against a yellowed plain like a pile of Texas tumbleweed. There'll be the black spike of the railroad running north-east, and a canal they got that men like to me built forty and more years ago. It kind of trickles in from the strict north.

Blakely   You saying army built it?

Trooper   Saying Irish built it. Irish toiled to dig it and many killed. Not much more than a ditch, not much more than a grave.

Blakely (*cheerfully*)   That be the ghost you mentioned?

Trooper (*blackly*)   How so, ghost?

Mo   That be how they be making a canal. With a tally of deaths, usual.

James   Railroad better than any water-road. I come north in America to see these marvels, and I see few enough of them – so far, so far. Give me gold, boys, and I might forsake them.

Nathaniel   I'll say a word for bridges, I did like the bridges of that Eastern coast. Looking like seagulls writ large, them good bridges sometimes – in the morning maybe. Bridge of Brooklyn. Mist rising around it, men blowing about with paint pots and new bolts up high in the summer.

James   But I'm finding – there be a pile of something better than bridges. Or them railroads or even glistening automobiles! Something I never went to find. Beauty somehow now and then. Here, North. Something easy in the airs. Aren't I better for being here? Maybe you don't know the days of Tennessee. Things there you finding. In a ditch out on a farmer's road, in yellow fields, in that half-done time of day. You might find a friend of your, the blood out on his face – I was thinking, you stay, James Miranda, and you be like that other James quite shortly, that had his head severed off, that was John's poor brother, in the fine, high days of the black book of Jesus. You best not stay so, James Miranda, were my words then.

Trooper *kicks his horse on. They all move into a bright clattering canter.*

Blakely What you want to do, Trooper? You want to skirt that wooded place?

Mo I thinking, you could catch a deer in that cover.

Blakely We a-deer hunting, Trooper?

A good local drumming music.

Trooper (*happily*) I am happy to hunt a deer there, quick.

Mo That be a silent serious animal – but I know her marks.

Nathaniel Wild boar more likely! Don't you understand Ohio? My pa's wild pigs – he got them on his Central Plains. That in Russia, boys!

Trooper Take our road through the wood!

Nathaniel Wild boar not rare in Brooklyn neither, gents!

Dark running green of trees. Sudden blind shadowiness. They duck the branches. Music.

Blakely Whoop! Man got to say, whoop! When he loving!

Nathaniel Pigs of Brooklyn, pigs of Brooklyn!

Trooper Fellas running! See them, Mo? Cross them, cross them, wedge them, boys!

Mo *slowly raises his rifle. A fresh light, a music. The others stilled. He rides with his head down, his body down. Up comes the gun. With a bleak dart of redness he fires the old gun. There's an earthly squeal.* **Mo** *stops his horse. The others surge down from their mounts and off to retrieve the boar.* **Mo** *watching on stage alone. Alert, sad. The others then bring on the dead boar – big, bristling.*

Blakely Heroes! That hunting!

Mo *pleased, quiet.*

Nathaniel Pretty bit of hunting, Blakely – that's true.

Trooper   Maybe we give up the trains and go businesslike for this. Jingo – don't they bleed? (*Trying to clean himself off.*)

They stop, just looking. Then **Nathaniel** *opens the neck-vein.*

Nathaniel   A fair-looker of a sow. A nice shapely girl.

James   Handsomest sow I ever saw. You see her on the beer sticker at home. Sow Brand Beer. Some things were wholesome!

Nathaniel   Sure was a fair-looker – considering . . .

Mo *rests his gun against himself with a certain air.*

Trooper (*putting a hand on* **Mo**'s *back lightly*)   Shooting, Mo.

Mo   Not so bad!

Trooper (*generally*)   I don't suppose any men ever had such a shooter in their midst.

Blakely   Speaking truth. That were (*searching for a good word*) a shot, Mo, a shot indeed. Looking like no one can shoot as sharp as an Amish boy of Ohio.

Nathaniel (*drawing his knife along the belly*)   Skinning, boys.

He sets to. **Blakely** *and* **James** *fix the fire. They put a pole through the boar and set her up across the fire.* **Blakely** *turns it about and about. Meanwhile* **Mo** *alone, looking at the work, rifle in hand. His own light. Music.*

Mo   A fly was sitting on his nose and it buzzing there and we were waking up in the bright room and Ezekiel looks down his nose at the fly and says, 'You go buzzing there, little fly, no harm to you.' And I was saying in my own sheets that he could do well to raise a hand to that daft creature and show the creation of flies that it weren't good to be sitting on the noses even of Amish folk and buzzing like that in the heat of the morning, and all the day of work before. And Papa drifting by outside in his black suit of linen with his beard as shapely as a spade, drifting the way he did, kind of disturbing the solid heat. And Ezekiel says that I was for roaming, since my thinking wasn't the likes of Papa's. And it wasn't. So in the morning a week following I shook Papa's hand and left him in the house. My brother came out on the track with me and gave me a blessing. He were an older man than me and he had a strong face and his hands and feet were big. He holds out his big hands and he says, 'Moses, you seem to be fixed on this going.' And I say, 'Zeke, it i'n't right for me to stay,' and he says, 'I think in all you're right there,' and he looks at me. Because he knew, once gone, he wouldn't see me again, since I couldn't return, no matter what befell me, according to our law. And that sun of morning was gold kind of like in his eyes, and I says, 'Zeke, it's a long road,' and he says, 'If ever you have a yearning for to scythe a sea of wheat, or to catch a roaming swarm and get that gold out of it, you know the place to come.' Well, he was lying then in his teeth. 'Zeke,' I says, 'thanks for the fresh pair of drawers and the Sunday hat,' I says, touching the rim of the hat as I spoke, and the gold just vanished out of his eyes because he turned away then. Zeke. It was the difference between wanting to kill that fly, and not killing it. And that was nigh on fifty year ago, in the brittle fields of North Ohio. I just weren't gentle like a proper Amish.

Blakely Come on, Mo Mason, and get your grub!

Mo *goes over and sits with them.*

Nathaniel (*holding something out in his fingers*) There you go, *Mr* Mason. (*Hands it to* **Mo**.)

Trooper That the killing bullet?

Nathaniel That's the one.

Mo *looking at it in his hand. Everything still. Light deepening to a clear burning sunset. A local music.* **Blakely** *slowly leans forward and turns the boar a last time. It's eaten away on the shown side. The light goes, the fire illuminates them now. They're replete with boar meat.* **Mo**'s *sitting with the rest.*

Nathaniel (*poking at his teeth with a twig, smelling his own breath*) Guess that sow was a garlic-eater.

Mo So a cook will say – a pig eats clean.

Nathaniel We won't see witches at this fire.

Blakely You think? I'm glad. Country sure looks bare and bleak about. This half-light's the time for them though and I seen big witches, big black dames about this time all over these states.

Trooper *sunken fearfully into himself.*

James That be marvels! What they do to you, Blakely?

Blakely Singing only.

James They was singing? What would they be singing, Blakely?

Blakely I don't know, Jim. They were singing though. Something like so . . . (*Tries a song.*) 'There were nine and ninety in the fold . . .'

Trooper I never seen a witch singing maybe, but I never seen a witch singing a hymn, if you follow me.

Blakely You not a witch-seeing man, Trooper. Some sees, some don't sees. You just a red-haired man and a red-haired man don't see much.

James I heard as much right enough – down South.

Blakely Fact, fact. Can't look a fact in the face and say it i'n't a fact. A fact stares right back. I wasn't intending to offend you, Trooper.

Trooper No – I don't mind not seeing witches.

Blakely So, some people would, see?

Trooper Not me, Blakely.

Blakely (*rising*) Any way I can take that glum out of you, Trooper? My, you getting to have an old man's manner of sitting. What's up with you?

Mo   Leave him be. He got the high dumps. It's a passing thing with us all. Less of the old man.

Blakely *standing nearer* **Trooper**.

Blakely   Maybe I can dance for you? Ever seen my dances?

Trooper (*looking up bleakly enough*)   Guess I have. None too pretty a sight.

Blakely   You thinking? (*Starts a waltz alone, hands high, leathers flapping, watching* **Trooper**.) Eh, eh? Footwork, footwork. Look and learn.

Trooper (*slight smile*)   Bear dances better, Blakely.

Nathaniel   Smells a damn sight better too.

Blakely   That's acause I han't got no partner.

Moves towards **Mo**.

Mo   Not on your black life, Blakely, you keep back from me.

James *and* **Nathaniel** *laughing, looking to* **Trooper**, **Trooper** *laughing now*.

Blakely   What about it, Missy Mo, maybe you care to shoot the leg?

Mo   Christ in his bed. I never saw the like. If I was a maiden, I'd surely cry. (**Blakely** *drags* **Mo** *up*.) God love you, leave an old man after a day of horses.

Blakely *stands before him formally, raises his hands to join* **Mo***'s, then ducks his hands down to button the edge of his coat back, in a flap to the side.*

James   Ah, that disgusting, Blakely.

Blakely   See, that what we used to do, to get a spur on them fillies . . .

Mo   Jesus Christ, Blakely, am going to spew!

Trooper *laughing now,* **Nathaniel** *strikes up a waltzing tune loudly.*

Blakely   Ready, my dove? (*He takes* **Mo***'s hands, starts to waltz him.*) Let's show the style now. (*They go a few steps.*) My, my, what a dainty little thing you are, Miss Mo. (**Nathaniel** *and* **James** *laughing hard,* **Trooper** *following.* **Blakely** *hits his crotch a couple of times against* **Mo***.*) Ha! Ha!

Trooper *away in laughter. They dance a little further.* **Trooper** *in deep laughter. They part, awkward, laughing, the others laughing, clapping.*

Blakely   Now, Trooper. I got you smiling.

Laughing again.

Trooper   Right. You did, Blakely.

Blakely *throws himself down, panting.* **Mo** *sits down carefully.*

Mo   Going to ache after that. (*They sit staring into the fire a moment, the moon has begun to rise behind.*) One time me and Trooper come into a bar-room in Texas. East Texas. We been two weeks deep country. Now we see the frost of money over people's eyes. But there was this fella standing stiff against the bar . . .

Trooper   I remember . . .

Blakely   I don't remember. Weren't I with you then?

Mo   Stiff against the bar, holding up the world you'd say – and he was roaring around at the clients saying, You the worst bunch of two-cent hustling no-hopes a man ever did see in America. And when we come in, he put it on worse, shouting at Trooper because of those old army pants, and giving out about the king of England and how America got rid of England when it suited her by God, and such items of history, and Trooper just turns and says, 'Mr, you need to scream, go ahead, we like screaming,' says he, 'we connoisseurs of screaming.' Educated, you know. 'Connoisseurs,' said the man, 'what you mean, some kind of song-birds, you meaning?' Ignorant, you know. And Trooper

says, 'No – but you stopped screaming. Scream some more!'
The man comes over and puts an arm about Trooper sort of
like in a music-hall skit, all friendly and joking, and he says,
'Fella, you a tomato.' Trooper says, 'You meaning, a peach?'
Man thinks for a moment and says, 'No, a tomato,' and
Trooper laughs. Trooper got a pleasant laughter. And that
was Blakely and how we met him.

Blakely *up again, looking around, gobsmacked.* **Nathaniel** *and*
James *enjoying it.*

Mo   Tomato!

Blakely   No, boys, no. Never was. I didn't remember that.
That right? You got me, Mo, you got me.

James *takes out a long clay pipe and fills it, things settle again. The*
moon well risen, a small spring moon. Smoke rises from **James**'s *pipe.*

James   What be the picking there on that train. Trooper?

Trooper   That fine train of ours we going to abuse? (**James**
nods.) Easter pay. Easter pay for the fort at Chagrin and
Bolivar – forts I should have said. That train going through
few days after that good and holy time. This time we're in
now, I should have said.

James   Gold – I might be a true man with gold in Ashville.
Gold can turn a human creature any colour. Make me shine.
Black with a gold shine. Could set up a gent in Ashville, with
that same gold. If a fella could bear the company. You did
say gold, Trooper?

Trooper   Part gold. Sides of beef, chuck, cornmeal, onions,
linen, hats, beans green, beans black, barley, whisky,
gunpowder, saltpetre, traps for varmints, bullets, bandages,
ribbons and eggs.

Nathaniel   For the Easter?

Trooper   How's that, Nathaniel?

Nathaniel   Easter eggs?

Trooper   Nope – hen's eggs.

Nathaniel   You know what I meaning by Easter eggs?

Trooper   I know what you meaning. You think the army sends Easter eggs to grown men in a gold train?

Nathaniel   I seen men as old as Mo getting eggs at the Easter-time in Brooklyn. That a Russian habit, boys.

Blakely   Darn fool Russians.

Trooper   Don't know rightly if I ever saw an Easter egg. I saw a duck's egg often enough, that a soft blue one, and one rare time I saw a heron's egg – hard to find. Sligo i'n't no fancy-dandy place like your Brooklyn. Children lucky to get dried ling at Christmas, leave alone eggs at Easter. Aister, we used to say. In my own house maybe you might have expected an egg, but I don't recall one. May be forgetting such things . . .

Nathaniel   Little painted eggs, Mo. You'd a liked them. Wood, kind of paper with flour water, a wild bird's egg.

Blakely (*in the background, vaguely to* **James**)   Lucky to get dried ling – that old shit of Trooper's . . .

Mo *smiles at* **Nathaniel**.

Trooper (*quietly singing*)   Eggs and eggs and marrowbones
                                                    Mix them all up well.
(*To himself.*) That's what we used to sing. Lucky to have eggs.

Blakely (*mockingly*)   Lucky to have bones, Trooper.

Nathaniel   You get the big noises in the churches at this time, in my Pa's town, out there in Russia. Prayers, blazing away. Old women singing like banditti and the gold everywhere. Big fellas with black beards doing the holy words. The name of that town, the name of that town . . . Snow would be gone then and the river eased out of its ice. There was this old white church across the watermeadows that old dead sailors built, you got big white-masted ships there in very old days, sails shrugging there among the fields and a deep river for the sea-going keels and that was two hundred miles inland. China merchants maybe, China bound. But the white church got lit with candles, three thousand and more, and you could stand on the meadows under the trees by the train station and look across at it, over the flooded meadows. That light burst out of it just the same as it was so much yellow water.

Blakely   How come you know that, Nathaniel, that never was in Russia? I assume you speaking about Russia?

Nathaniel   I seeing through my Pa's eyes now for you. See, I shut my own, and seeing through his.

Blakely   You got your father's eyes in there under your lids?

Nathaniel   I hope so.

Blakely   I don't know if you a crazy Russian sometimes.

Nathaniel   No, crazy come from my Ma – she were a Chinee. She used to say, herself in America, like a wingless bird in the Land of Fire.

James (*suddenly, mostly to himself*)   We don't got molasses, salt beef, Mex beans or flat-bread flour – five prime vittals – and we don't got one of them!

Mo   On the morrow, Jim, as much store-buying as you like. Maybe we could be for turning in now.

Trooper   Someone got to go down to the brook and fill the nose-sack with fresh water for them horses there. Otherwise, they'll break their tethers towards dawn. Indians will get them for sure.

Blakely   No Indians now, Trooper. You surely shot them all.

Trooper   Never could shoot an Indian.

Blakely   Well – that what the Yankee government were paying you for. Weren't you in all them Indian wars in the eighties? You said so.

Trooper   I said I was in them since I was. Still wearing the duds, hah? Didn't say never that I was shooting Indians.

Nathaniel   Why didn't you shoot them, Trooper? You had an employment there to shoot Indians. You the only one of us ever held a proper employment, aside from breaking stones. You should have shot a few for the look of things.

Trooper   Be like shooting you, Nathaniel. You ever see a true Indian place? Don't mean the places they give them now. Don't mean where the missionary men have them cooped now and giving them new words and shirts, and trying to get them to look dandy and plough and not be drinking and stabbing. Ever see an Indian town – the tent towns? (**Nathaniel** *uncomprehending*.) Put me in mind of certain Sligo hills, and certain men in certain Sligo hills. The English had done for us, I was thinking, and now we're doing for the Indians. You asking Trooper why he never killed? I *seen* plenty killed, I don't say I didn't. Girls hiding in brushwood, taken for a soldier's violent pleasure. Brothel and butcher shop. Well – didn't seem . . . Unless you been to war you don't . . . These weren't fellas drinking all day and churched at Sunday . . . These were (*smiling*) oh, characters. We'd go in and have to . . . You couldn't leave nothing alive. You know.

Mo   That years back, Trooper. Lord love you, that years back.

Trooper   Yeh. Who'll fetch the water?

Blakely   Here (*taking the sack*), I do it. (*Looking down at* **Trooper**.) Guess we weren't there, Trooper.

He goes to fill water from the brook. The others settle into their blankets, grunting and shifting. Scratching. **Blakely** *crosses to the horses with the water-sack. They make stamping noises, whinnies to see him.* **Blakely** *chuckles.*

Blakely   Thirsty men, i'n't ye? You want some more trickling water, Mr Thunder? Keep you fresh for speed tomorrow, boy. Never shot an Indian! He think I believing him? He were a full-pay Trooper then – a-course he shot himself Indians. Probably shot whole towns of them. I bet all that glistening gold in that train, I bet it all that what he

says there i'n't true. Hold up, Queenie, hold up, you'll get
your share. Because, his face look like he shot them . . . I
know how them Irish are where Trooper come from. Savage
they living. Han't got shoes. Han't got food most of them.
Eating nettles and prayers I'll be bound. Lucky to have
bones, Trooper! I seen Irish like that, holed up in the
crevices of America just as cockroaches do, or the very lice
on my body, and I never saw an Indian as bad as an Irish. I
didn't. Maybe just nearly as bad. Maybe the same. I'm
betting he shot his fair share. Why wouldn't an Irish shoot
an Indian? Trooper shot thousands. Shot more Redmen than
King Buffalo, I'm saying. What you think, Mr Thunder?
And they had buffalo too up there in those damned Sligo
hills, till the Irish ate them, raw from the hoof up. You want
to get wisdom, Trooper, talking to Blakely. Blakely knows.
(*The horses whinny.*) What frights you, boys, what frights you?

In the darkened camp, **Trooper** *wakes suddenly. He gives a cry.*

Mo   Easy, easy, child.

Trooper   I an't no fearful child, Mo.

The trees silver now in the moon, **Blakely** *silvered.*

Mo   Why don't you bring your blanket a shade nearer to
me, Trooper?

Trooper   You say I might, Mo?

Mo   A shade, a shade.

Trooper *a little closer.*

Trooper   What was I doing here in wide America?

Mo   Sleeping, sleeping. Not like me. (**Trooper** *asleep again
nearly.*) I'm wide awake in wide America.

Act Two

Clear morning, the men packing up their horses. The fire only a black mark on the clay. **Mo** *stamping it out firmly.* **Trooper** *by him and the other three nearly mounted and ready.*

Mo One time I was in Kansas droving hogs for a syndicate. Long before I met you. Through the yellow gullies of Kansas. One morning I catch a change in the weather, by the way those hogs kept stopping and looking round for holes, caves, and such – well. Shortly up the country comes, comes walking, a fury of a dust cloud, tornado, ripping up plantings yonder, stirring through the great blue – in a fury. Saddest single thing I ever saw – the anger of that twisting wind. Disturbing where farmers had things set. The lack of use in it. Not a plougher or a planter, nor a drover. Empty-headed anger. Saddest thing. But, the hogs two steps ahead of it.

Trooper (*moving with* **Mo** *towards the horses*) You want me (*putting his rifle in its holder*) to be more like them hogs, Mo?

Mo Don't sit so raw up in the wind, maybe.

Blakely Heading out, fellas. What time on your fob-watch, Trooper?

Trooper (*drawing it out, looking, shaking it, listening to it*) The hands is stuck or stopped.

Blakely You sat on it, Trooper, maybe.

Trooper Wharf-watch. My father timed ships by it and tides and workings of men.

Mo Who'll need a timepiece while the sun shines and the moon?

Trooper All right. (*Mounting.*) Suits me just as fine.

Blakely (**Mo** *mounting nimbly*) You i'n't so stiff, after dancing!

Mo Morning, noon, evening, night – those things are there if you have a timepiece or not.

Riding through green shadows. **Blakely** *more dressed in light, riding, excited.*

Blakely You i'n't so stiff, Mo Mason, you i'n't so stiff. You flush with life! Never will get tired of the motley bushes of America! Any wilderness suits Blakely. There were nine and ninety in the fold! And one was lost – shepherd got himself scratched by briars *(shading his eyes with one hand)* looking for his ransomed Blakely! Better and more life than my old faither. Faither, toilsome, hardy, a black rabbit, a dark stoat, a velvet-jacketed mole. And all about the white streets lay the dust of his mines, heaping, holding, hardening, till the clear granite of Lincolnshire turned to basalt and hellstone, and the trout-flying streams coiled bleakely about dead dogs and debris of love, and the crest of the King withered from the wall of the town hall, and my faither found his age, and we threw him down into the soil, and we felt the soil shake under our shoes, and his soul thundered into the disused tunnels, and someone cast after him a pleasant rose! *(Up in his stirrups now, streaming.)* More life, Mo, more life!

Mo's *great cry! They ride in fast unison, music. A flail of travelling. The attitudes of their faces, the style of their riding, painterly, eyes lost to the movement. Sunlight breaks over them in falls of gold. They dismount, looking down on White Woman Street.*

Mo That a fair-looking town.

Trooper White Woman Street. She grown a little right enough. Hard to make out the waterways now. Canal must be sneaking out there behind those red roofs. Town's mopping it up.

Mo Queer-named spot.

Trooper Yep, got its name from that famous girl used to see to business here. Only white woman for five hundred miles of wilderness.

Blakely You say so, Trooper?

Trooper   Canal builders used to spend majorities of their wages on that woman. Every step west you forgot what beauty of women was, till you hit White Woman Street and that sweat-drenched withered girl was more perfect than first love. All Ireland's emigrants knew that furrow, and set their seeds against her, but I expecting nothing grew. If you was poor or lost your bills in cards, you shacked with an Indian. That time Indian weren't said to be even just a human person, but a kind of running hare or doe – fellas said they were going to rut a deer since money was fresh lost. One old sailor, who had lain with dolphins, as sailors sometimes do, said dolphins were more pleasing to him than any Indian girl. And what was they that spoke but local Irish eels lost and growing in that Sargasso sea? They was simpler times and it seemed the same to me and all I wished was to see that white woman and be her cash lover.

Nathaniel   Ever rise to such dignity?

Trooper   I nearly.

Blakely   I knew you did.

Trooper   How you say, Blakely?

Blakely   I knew you did go in – any Christian man would have.

Trooper   Well – went in to her by God one time when flush with cash. My troop brought in two hundred scalps and we were bonus. I had my token in my hand as good as gold, a little tin plate with a star on it, and she was there, Nathaniel, kind of saying nothing in the dark. Oh, I was, I was young, you know? But I catched my arm in her shabby curtains as I passed and what I did see shocked my poor soul.

Blakely   Pox, was it, Trooper? Woman like that, lying down with mere Irish?

Trooper   It weren't nothing of that kind, Blakely. It were a devious trick out of the wilderness. Weren't she like a saint to

those men, a place for pilgrimage. Tober nAlt she was, a
holy well, a shrine, St Bridget, some powerful class of folk
that would bring you luck and ease your longing?

Blakely   God-damned street-woman sounds to me.

James   Shush, Blakely. Trooper remembering.

Trooper   I sounding like a fool, I know that, Blakely. I
were seeing her in light, like no man before me, by grace of
hooking part of me in a curtain. I'd a chose the darkness!

Nathaniel   Was it age, Trooper?

Trooper   Age? She had no age to mention. Less than you.
Just a girl. With two circles of rouge on her cheeks and her
wild green eyes lost as emeralds in a Texas stream. Never
seed a child so frighted, holding out her arms to me, as if to
shut my eyes, a dusty pilgrim that had walked some twenty
miles to give her my best coin. No one could ever measure
that need I feeling, a boy sullied up by wars, Indian wars.
That need to view a sight of home, a goddess of my own
countrymen. Men from my troop had swore she was from
Listowel! You don't know that town – a little city of Ireland.
But, boys, the dark of the room was her only whiteness, and
in the light of day she was one so lovely Indian girl, a
sparkling doe, a hare bright in the haggard, a hunter's
reproach.

Mo   Guess that white woman were dead or old and they
liked to keep that trade.

Blakely   I do hope you whupped her, Trooper.

James   Whupping don't answer, Blakely.

Trooper   Was all that pay and dreaming of my countrymen
I thinking of, those farms they left when food got scarce,
those long black nights aboard the famous ships, their arms
pushing spades and hauling up axes in America, digging and
cutting like pigs and dogs, men whose children had froze in
ditches, brothers died with that green about their lips, the

smear of nettles, whose religion was washed clear out of them by hunger – clear, tested, cursing men that no one could wager was worth two farts, filthy flotsam of Ireland, letterless, stumbling, crooked men that had nothing to believe on but that there were one white woman here, a woman of a hundred stories, a hundred boasts, a kind of fire-hot legend of those days, such as had power over their talk and in truth, boys, let me say it, was likely a goddess, and surely built that canal.

Blakely   Makes a man wonder though.

Trooper   What wondering?

Blakely   How's you coming back here.

Trooper   Why coming back? Because I know about that train, and gold of that train has me sitting on my black-assed horse there. (**Nathaniel** *laughs*.)

Nathaniel   Maybe we ride down now, where them poor Irish got duped?

Blakely   I got to say it, Trooper, but an English wouldn't hunt rabbit in the dark.

Trooper   Well. We know our duty, boys. Where we stop first in town we know.

Blakely   We know? (*Mounting*.)

Nathaniel   You saying whorehouse? Our duty in the whorehouse? (*To* **Mo**.) Yes, sir.

Trooper   Not there first, Nathaniel. What we do ever first in a sweet town?

Nathaniel   Forgetting.

Trooper   You follow after me. Then you remember your duty. We camp on that lower hill, you see that section, and walk down from there. Go down, Queenie, go down.

*The stage dark with glints of gold, specks of iconry here and there.
The men have exited. A dark cloth over the horses.*

Blakely (*off*)   What class of a chapel this be?

James (*off*)   Baptist, Blakely.

Blakely (*off*)   Whoah!

James (*off*)   What difference?

Blakely (*off*)   None, none . . .

*They come on respectfully in the half-light. They strike their breeches
to get the dust off.* **Nathaniel** *raises his hat and smoothes back his
hair. The other hats are removed in a chain reaction.* **Trooper** *kneels
on one knee, hat held there, other hand over his head, Irish fashion.
They pray vigorously.* **Nathaniel**, *and* **Mo** *in his Amish fashion, out
loud.*

Nathaniel   Nathaniel he wicked – can't see the good in
Nathaniel. Here because Trooper say we should – he right. I
was thinking only of – that wicked house a-down the
street . . .

Mo   More love!

Nathaniel   Maybe, maybe you should pour some of that
hellfire down on it, only – maybe spare the girls.

Blakely (*glancing at* **Trooper**)   That be prayers?

Trooper   Good as any else. Got some of your own, han't
you, Blakely?

Blakely   Acres of them – acres.

Trooper   Pray them so . . .

Nathaniel   Nathaniel Yeshov is a Brooklyn man and what
they pray in Russia he forget. What prayers of China he
never knew, though some day, in that land of fire . . .
Forgetting a deal of things. Wilderness do that, mister.
Scatter the thoughts of a simple man. Maybe you look out

for me. You know the truth of me I guess – see it all. Sad picture.

Mo　More love!

Nathaniel　Well, thanking you, mister.

He gets up, looks down at the others, taps his hat. **James** *unexpectedly begins.*

James　That was Jimmy's luck to meet these boys. The arms of these men have cradled me, given me a place to rest, a kind of home, though we moving our home day to day. For these boys I be willing to hang, to fester in prison, to take the fall. When I run first I run out to see the marvels of America, that was my wish. I had seen the dead part long enough. Ashville i'n't no paradise of ease and I was told by many that in the North you could walk careless, even so far after the bitter lies of that war. Richmond. So out I run to see them marvels of America and here I am to note it down and praise it. These four men have shown me the free silver of all daybreaks, the shrug of grass when it growing across a hundred acres, freely and finely, and shown me that a heart's friend don't cause too many aches, but heals the hurt of many old ones, with a bit of laughter, and easiness I wasn't used to knowing. And if that muddy slough bar my way, they shown me how to leap it. Careless! This world can throw what it might at me, but I am among the beauties of America with these friends, and we are mighty enough in it, and are pleased. It i'n't work for angels, what we doing, so we don't sing innocent, but say we done it all, we done all that, because we are robbermen that know our work and know the beauties of America.

Nathaniel *tries to see back into the gloom.*

Nathaniel　Thanking you too, padre!

James (*rising*)　That not the padre, Nathaniel. That just a statue.

Nathaniel　Dark in this holy place, Jim.

James　We go the store now, Trooper?

Trooper (*rising, confused*)   Sure, Jim. (*After a little.*) Seen an eatery corner of this street. (*Smiling.*) Some good Ohio food make new men of us.

Mo   Ohio grub, believe me, cattle grits and longshadow beef – lead on, Trooper.

Blakely *makes a face to* **Nathaniel**. *They go off upstage left. The white dusty sunlight of the street outside.* PATS BEST EATS *written over a door. The men come back out by it.* **James** *with a sack of provisions.*

Blakely (*reading the sign*)   Pat's God-damned Best Eats. Merciful Christ. Them beans was like chewing little river stones.

Nathaniel   I couldn't eat, what with paradise at hand.

Bar counter swings in.

Mo (*rubbing his stomach*)   Going to nurse that beef all night. Still moving, one way or another.

Blakely *standing nearer the bar counter, light of the whorehouse there growing, displacing the street.*

Blakely   El Dorado, boys – God's heaven!

They herd into the poorly lit room.

Mo   Quiet for a place of joy. This the same old place you spoke of, Trooper?

Trooper   Could be, could be. Everything looking very different. But, maybe so.

An old man comes out, an Indian, **Clarke**, *dressed much the same as themselves.*

Mo   You know that old man?

Trooper   I never seen that old man.

Clarke   You want women, boys – or what?

Mo   We want women. Well – these fellas want them. Me, I want a woman, but couldn't locate no bathhouse, and I reckon I smell too high. These other gents been soaping in innocent rivers betimes. I could never abide open-air washing.

Clarke   Women in there, dollar each. We don't want no biting and no fighting.

Mo   Right. Now, boys. No biting and no fighting. (**Nathaniel**, **James** and **Blakely** *file out upstage centre*.) Right. So, Trooper, you?

Trooper *staring after the others*.

Trooper   No – just later. Drop of whisky down here, mister, meantime.

Trooper *stands at lonelier end of the bar,* **Mo** *moves to* **Clarke**, *the bar between them.* **Mo** *sets his hat on the bar,* **Clarke** *puts whisky by* **Trooper**, *silently asks if* **Mo** *wants some.*

Mo   No, sir. Never did touch it. Only bit of religion ever stuck.

Trooper *drinks,* **Mo** *and* **Clarke** *quiet for the moment.*

(*After a bit.*) You mind me asking, mister, what that shiny thing be there? (*Pointing to a locket around* **Clarke**'s *neck*.)

Clarke   This here? What you think it is?

Mo   Is what I'm asking.

Clarke   My mother, you want to know.

Mo   Now you surprise me, mister.

Clarke   Can't buy it.

Mo   No, that understood, that understood.

Clarke   Ashes of her head only, sorry to report. Soldier's woman at Gettyburg. First bombardment, she serving the officers their chuck, big shell lobbed over, explosion, mother gone. They find her head, cremate it. (*Holds out locket.*) Death of a good woman. Only good woman in this town.

Mo   That a grievous violent death, mister.

Clarke I'n't nothing to these parts. Fellas knocking each other down in Ohio all day. Considered a pleasantry to stab someone. Like a compliment. See it here on pay days. I had two murders here on that very floor. And years ago, when there were no civilisation going at all, some fool killed a woman here.

Mo That was low work.

Clarke You're saying. Fella drew his knife across her throat, just like she was a pig to bleed. Happened in there, one of the rooms.

Mo Man caught?

Clarke Caught? Lawless days. Anyways, he never was caught. And she weren't no bad woman neither. Better call her a girl – sixteen, little Ohio river girl, not like me. I hail from the Smoky Mountains myself. Little Indian girl – came up from the river somewhere, like they used to then. She done her best to get by and some disgraceful man he do her in.

Mo You never see him again, that murdering man?

Clarke Never seen him in the first place. I weren't officially connected to this premises at that time. Scouting for army then, I was. Some other poor man standing here. Old negra man, I remember him, in those early days, and another Indian that still wore crow's feathers in his head, and carried his hair longer than the preacher would let you now. And spoke no English words – not like me doing here – easy as white man.

Mo You got damn good English, mister, damn best of that English I been hearing these seventy years of my life. I hear many men gabbling English and you the best at it. You riding the best pony of English I seen.

Blakely (*off*) Whoop!

Clarke Thank you, mister. That's kind. My name just Clarke, you want to know.

Mo   I meaning it, that complimenting I was doing to you. Name's Mo Mason, I were born in Ohio and have wandered extensive since them days . . . (*About to shake* **Clarke***'s hand, but* **Blakely** *reappears.*) Well, Blakely. Didn't expect you so soon. (**Blakely** *strides over between* **Mo** *and* **Trooper**.) You looking like the cat that got the milk. (**Blakely** *puts an arm on* **Mo***'s back, leans towards* **Trooper**.)

Blakely   Whooooo, Trooper.

Trooper   Don't trouble me, Blakely.

Blakely   Trouble you? No, sir. (*Turning to* **Mo**.) I can recommend that, Mo Mason. Any man could rise nimble after that. (**Nathaniel** *and* **James** *coming out.*) Look at these boys of paradise. Step over, boys, if you can still move your legs, and take whisky with Blakely. (**Clarke** *serves them.*) There's your three dollars, mister, and a dollar for what whisky we can drink.

Clarke   Sure.

Blakely   Why don't you give us your song, Mo? The Mighty Ohio. Ah, that a good song, Mo.

Mo   Singing regular, Mr Clarke?

Clarke   No biting and no fighting. But singing's regular.

Mo *shapes himself to sing.*

Blakely   That's it.

James   Shush, Blakely. Mo fixing to sing.

Mo   I singing 'bout the mighty Ohio
that flowing through this sweet land
Working men are seeing her and saying
she soft and white like a maiden's hand

The men listening.

Ohio she bring water to the harvest
making corn and tobacco plant grow

But that i'n't nothing to the drifter
he just like how her white waters flow

Nathaniel *quietly joins in.*

Mo *and* **Nathaniel**

Maybe he left his sweet home lately
where the honeysuckle twine by the door
He feeling the calling of the Ohio River
and whole wide America what's more

Blakely *gently takes the arm of* **James** *and brings him out from the bar and dances with him. The voices of* **Mo** *and* **Nathaniel** *flow freely now.* **Trooper** *alone buried into himself.*

Man he can pray to the mighty Ohio
to bring him to a sweet place at last
where he be finding a wife for to nurture
and throw his old grief to the past

Blakely *and* **James** *awkwardly stop. They're silent for a few moments.* **Blakely** *by the 'door'.*

Blakely   Night's fallen.

Clarke   That right singing, Mr Mo, and done me good to hear about that Ohio River. (*Lighting candle.*)

Nathaniel   You wouldn't find a singer finer on Coney Island itself.

Blakely   What you saying, Trooper? (**Trooper** *glances across at him, frightened.*) Eggs and eggs and marrowbones! Be drinking with your pals!

Mo   Blakely, Blakely, how long I know you?

Blakely   Me, Mo? How long you know Blakely? You know Blakely five year this Eastertime – no, sir, this first May coming.

Clarke   Easter a good time in the world. Preacher worn out by this time, telling the business in the chapel – I hear him myself, all last week.

Blakely   Now, what a whorehouse injun doing in the blessed chapel?

Mo   Blakely, in them long five years, I ever ask you to clam up a piece?

Blakely (*innocently*)   Not that I recollect, Mo. You want me to . . . Sure. A little more whisky. That be it. I be just minding to myself what happened in yonder, just recent. I understand you. I ain't a fool. Not this Blakely.

Nathaniel   Guess I missed Easter proper. The Sunday and all, and the hanging on the Friday. I'n't that the road for you? Missed the thing. Where we are I don't know half the time, summer, Easter. You think it was prison the way I be in the head betimes. But, here's to freedom, boys!

They drink.

All *but* **Trooper** *and* **Clarke**   To freedom.

Blakely   Blakely die if he ever see the gates opening again for him. If ever you see them leading Blakely to the cells, and you have a gun, you have a knife, shoot Blakely, stab him down – he don't want to live!

Blakely *collapses.*

Nathaniel   I shoot him now if he likes.

Clarke   Your friend shipshape?

Mo   Pay no heed. Two drinks always knocks down Blakely. That's how an English drinks, I guess. You best carry him, Nathaniel, since you slayed him. (**Nathaniel** *lifting him up and across one shoulder.*) Be thankful you a free man and don't be mentioning no prison out here where we happy to forget such places and do our work like respectable men.

Nathaniel *heads off with* **Blakely**.

James   Russia carrying England, Mo. What's bothering Trooper? He don't laugh, he don't sing.

Mo   Don't know, Jim.

James   You be bringing him along?

Mo   He i'n't pie-eyed, he just quiet. You go with Nathaniel, case he drops that varmint.

James   Oh, she were such a sweet woman.

Mo   Who, Jim?

James   In there, Mo.

He follows after **Nathaniel,** *and off.*

Clarke   You and your friend got a few minutes?

Mo   Sure. Don't we, Trooper?

Trooper   Sure.

Clarke   Can you do a man a favour, Mr Mo? (*Drawing out a newspaper from his coat.*) Don't mean to presume on our friendship so far.

Mo   I can. (*Takes newspaper.*) *White Woman Street Gazette and Advertiser.* You want me to . . .

Clarke   I like to get the news. Business slow tonight or I could get a regular to read it to me. I don't know what it is, but when I hear the happenings of the world I am contented.

Mo   Kind of starved for news myself. You just got the front part here, Clarke, or maybe there i'n't much news around here. Well . . .

Clarke   What is it?

Mo   Garters, 50c.

Clarke   Oh, good. Well, tell you the truth, Mr Mo, I don't wear stockings.

Mo   Me neither, Clarke. You desire me to read some item?

Clarke   Why don't you? Lord Jesus, I enjoy it.

Mo   Big fellas here, they say three men took for some robbery – they was hanged anyhow.

Clarke   That how they put it?

Mo   No. Allan gang hanged, would be what they have here.

Clarke   Allan gang hanged. That really something. What they do, Mr Mo?

Mo   Says, see page three. We ha'n't got page three, Clarke. Some devilment of poor outlaws, I expect. (*After a bit.*) That war there in Europe i'n't doing the boys of England much good – so this saying. Great tally of deaths . . .

Clarke (*expectant*)   Yes?

Mo   Says, see page seven. Well (*handing back paper*), that's the height of it, leaving aside corsets and such.

Clarke   I sure like to get the news.

Mo   All right, Trooper?

Trooper   We shift if you want, Mo.

Mo (*to* **Clarke**)   Well . . . (*Setting his hat on his head.*)

Trooper   We got everything, Mo? Ah, hell. Did Jim have that fool sack of his?

Mo   Good thinking. I don't think he did. You see our friend carry his sack?

Clarke   The negra? Don't recall it. Must have left it where he was. (*To* **Trooper**.) You go in and fetch it, girls won't have touched it – they sitting out on the veranda now, with the slow business, drinking chicory – I hear them chattering. Take the candle in. It be dark in there. Take them moths and the squeeters with you . . .

Mo   You want to go, Trooper?

Trooper   I can't go, Mo. I can't go in there.

Clarke   I'n't nobody there, mister.

Trooper   I couldn't. I thinking I could and I couldn't. Mo, I thinking I could. But we'll leave that sack.

Mo   I go. (*Holding the candle.*) Can't leave Jim's store-bought vittals. What would he think of us. Be angered with us.

Mo *goes upstage,* **Trooper** *watching hard.* **Mo** *disappears into the inner brothel, taking the light with him. There's the glimmer of it* *filling the doorway.* **Trooper** *and* **Clarke** *left in the dark more or less,* **Trooper***'s eyes fixed on the changeable light.*

Clarke   What you afeard of, mister? Just a few rooms in there.

Trooper   Nothing. Just ghosts maybe. Just old ghosts.

Clarke   My grandpa he saying that moths and such be the spirits of the dead ones. If you quiet now you can hear them banging the window glass to get back out to the moon. You hear them? No. Maybe they follow Mr Mo. My grandpa saying that but I saying they just nuisances, catching in your face and burning theyselves. (**Trooper** *staring.*) Where you from, mister?

Trooper   Where from? Ireland.

Clarke   I knew. We get plenty Irish in here. Place there burning like Richmond, I hear. Some big mail depot or someplace. Fire and ruin in Dublin. Fellas put in jail and likely to be shot. Fighting the English.

Trooper (*not listening, fixed on the door*)   That right?

Clarke   So I hear. I sure like to get the news. Fighting the English. My grandpa fighting the English too. English won. You ever hear tell of them Indian wars? A-course you did.

Trooper   He gone a long time.

Clarke   He dead a long time right enough. Virginia.

Trooper   I meaning Mo is.

Clarke   It dark in there. (*Light growing again in the doorway.*) Here he is. (**Mo** *emerges. Brushes away a white moth.*)

Trooper   What you see?

Mo   I didn't see nothing but this sack, Trooper. (**Mo** *sets down the candle.*) Look, thanking you, Mr Clarke, for all your kindness.

Clarke   All right, Mr Mo.

Trooper *fixed.* **Mo** *takes his arm.*

Mo   Come on, Trooper. Whisky has you spooked.

Mo *and* **Trooper** *go out together into the starlight,* **Trooper** *remembering to lift his hand silently in farewell to* **Clarke**, **Clarke** *likewise.*

Clarke   Good journey, mister.

After a bit **Trooper** *stops in the shadowy street.*

Mo   We want to get along, seeing as the boys are waiting for us.

Trooper   Where we going now anyhow?

Mo   Just up there that ways, outside of town. Boys are waiting for us.

Trooper *nods.*

Trooper   A-course we are. A-course we are. I like the boys. That was a sweet song you sang, Mo. Don't think I weren't listening. I heard you and what you meaning. Sometimes, don't we all wonder why we left home where we were known and came out to see these plains and towns? We do.

Mo   This be the closest I been to home in forty years. But it still too far to go.

Trooper   Mo, I come back to White Woman Street to see if maybe Trooper O'Hara can wipe the slate clean and go back to being what he was.

Mo   You don't need to say nothing to me about that.

Trooper   That because you a king of men, Mo. You saying your brother Ezekiel more of a king than you? No, no. Maybe Mo you hear dark things from that Indian Clarke and you thinking about me?

Mo *looking at* **Trooper**, *thinking, going back over what Clarke said. He remembers, almost steps back from* **Trooper**.

Mo   I know better than I know my own boots that you never kill no woman like that . . .

Trooper   See, Mo, and if you did think it, you would be saying nothing, and when I was waking up sudden in the night you wouldn't scorn to comfort me.

Mo   Because I seeing you as my brother, Trooper, and a man don't care to think too dark about his brother.

Trooper   I'm going to tell you now, Mo Mason, so you won't need to put this from your mind and just be Trooper's innocent brother. I didn't kill her like they said she was done, but I killed her just the same, no matter what mighty judge say different. She were an Indian girl pretty as the dawn with emerald eyes like a wolf's and I bedded her. And I looks down after and that woman is bleeding the way a first-time woman does, and she not crying in her face but I see the thing worse than tears, that dry and fearful look. A lost look. Then fast as a wolf she dips down to take my cold English blade from my breeches belt, and dragged it flashing like a kingfisher across her throat. She dragged it with force. Jesus of the world, I couldn't put her together again, Mo, she had a waterfall coming from her wound, and making a sound of water too. She just choked and died in front of me.

Mo   Trooper, you didn't kill that poor lonesome girl.

Trooper   I just run like a rabbit.

Mo   Why ever you come back, Trooper?

Trooper   Well, I don't know. I don't know why I left home and I don't know why I come back to White Woman Street. I thought, if I was in that room again, I could say something to her, I could do something kinder.

Mo   But she dead thirty years, Trooper.

Trooper   I know, I know she dead. I don't know what I was . . . Couldn't look at them girls tonight. Couldn't go into the room. Couldn't recall the look of the place hardly . . .

Mo   Trooper, this world be darker than a mine for sin and hurt, but I saying to you, Trooper, without a lie, that you still lighting well enough, you still a man deserving life and a

measure of happiness, in spite of all. You carried that poor
girl a long way and time now you laid her down gentle and
let her be buried where maybe she don't belong, but any field
of the earth be good for such a sleep. What happen in
America is like a rover flood, everything lifted and dragged
away from its place. Not just Trooper hurt by this flood and
I'm telling you, Trooper, that rain of America i'n't your
doing.

Mo *pulls the dark cloth off the 'horses'. Early morning sunlight floods
the stage. The three other men just waking.* **Mo** *moves upstage.*
Blakely *shakily out of his blanket.*

Blakely   Whoah. (*Seeing* **Trooper**.) Trooper?

Trooper   Yes, Blakely?

Blakely   Trooper, I offend you?

Trooper   No, Blakely.

Blakely *goes to* **Trooper**, *puts an arm on his shoulder.*

Blakely   I offend you in that whorehouse and not know
how I was dong it because I be a God's fool?

Trooper   No.

Blakely   Trooper, you a peach.

Trooper   You meaning a tomato?

Blakely   No, a peach.

James *rises quite nimbly from his blanket.* **Blakely** *heads back to
pack his gear up.*

(*Surprised.*) Morning, Mr Lazarus!

James *fixing the fire and the coffee.* **Mo** *trailing back past*
Trooper. **Mo** *looking at something in his hand.*

Trooper   Sun up maybe these twenty minutes. Train
coming in below the sun. When we see the sun half-risen we
be near that freight of gold. (**Mo** *nods pleasantly.*)

James (*fixing the coffee*)   If she's there.

Nathaniel (*still in his blanket*)   She'll be there. And don't mind if she there or not. I feel just a lifetime of fine trains ahead of me. I'm going to pick the innards of every train from here to Argentina in this allotted span. (*Rising up.* **Mo** *by him.*)

Mo   See this, Nathaniel.

Nathaniel (**Mo** *hands him something*)   What's this, Mo?

Mo   Found it under my hand in the grasses. In that deep dry grass. I can't say what colour you call that. Kind of speckled anyhow. (**Nathaniel** *peering at it.*)

Nathaniel   That's kind of you, Mo. Why for giving it to me?

Mo   Easter egg. Russian Easter egg.

The men gather for the coffee. **Blakely** *takes a slug from his cup.*

Blakely   What man in creation but Jim Miranda could make Blakely feel better after whisky?

James   You feel better?

Blakely   Nope, but . . .

They laugh.

Nathaniel   And who carried you home, Blakely?

Blakely   Who carried me?

Nathaniel   Why you think my back's broke?

Blakely   All your sinning.

They laugh.

Trooper   We're mounting up now. We're going. In fine fettle and with the best intentions.

The fling their dregs into the fire. A local music. They mount up. The freshening sun. Cantering now. Their faces eager and happy. Age falls away. The gold frost of the sun opens the sky, opens the woods and the hearts. The train is heard now in the distance, it blows its whistle as it

passes through White Woman Street. They ride, the train's noise
increases, it rushes upon them, the sky engoldens, and suddenly they are
under the mass of the golden train, rushing and Leviathan.

Blakely   Trooper, Trooper, that be the golden train herself!

Trooper   Train of redemption, boys, ride for that train of
redemption!

Nathaniel   Redemption for Brooklyn, boys, for Russia!

James   Redemption for the beauties of America!

In that moment fire opens up from the train, there's a mingling of
smoke and steam and shouting. The gold fades into darkness. When
things clear, the horses and the men are gone. Only **Blakely** *on his*
own in gold light.

Blakely   Blakely be alone. One time Blakely was a Grimsby
lad and talked good Grimsby talk but he lost all them words.
That good shepherd, scratched though he be by briars, still
can't find Blakely. Now he speaks like a mighty American,
he got the lingo of the mighty Ohio, humming and hawing in
that Yankee fashion. Let me tell you a tale. We had no food
for eating which is why I was leaving Grimsby. Some years
before me other Grimsby men left Grimsby. Wild, religious-
minded men that called each other Father and the
womenfolk Mother and such. What they do, they rose into
America – leaving Grimsby and rose into America. Now
Blakely don't recall his own first name. But he do recall
where those long-dead travellers left from, same place he left
from years after, and what was the name of the place.
Blakely couldn't forget such a good name, such a fine name,
and it still in his head, singing to Blakely, though Blakely
don't ever know which way to go – Killinghome Creek,
Killinghome Creek.

His light gone. In normal daylight, **Mo** *comes on helping* **Trooper**,
whose chest is stained with blood.

Mo   You still hurting, Trooper?

Trooper   You see the others?

Mo   I seen Jim and Nathaniel going like hares for the wilderness.

Trooper   And Blakely?

Mo   Didn't see Blakely. He were more nearer the train.

Trooper   Safe if I rest up here a little while?

Mo   Safe enough here, Trooper.

Trooper   Just a share of sleep. (*Eyes closed.*) I seeing that shining hawthorn, Mo, you seeing it?

Mo   I seeing it. Go on, you sleep. I'll hunker here by you. You sleep, Trooper. May your eyes not see me, Trooper. May your eyes see the hawthorns of home. Look, Trooper. See the dances? Old rattling dances? (*Raising his arms slightly.*) More love, Trooper, more love. Look, Trooper – Ireland.

He looks off, raising his gun slowly in his fashion. A local music.

Dark-suited men coming up the hill to us, Trooper. Who they be? That you, Jimmy? That you, boys?

Blakely, *with* **Nathaniel** *and* **James**.

Blakely   A-course it is.

Nathaniel *and* **James** *look down at* **Trooper**. **Blakely** *kneels to him*.

Who else it be? Not those fool guards.

Mo (*after a bit*)   Jees Christ . . .

Blakely   No. Jees Christ don't walk in these woods.

Music. Dark. Curtain.